# CONTENT

|   | Introduction | |
|---|---|---|
|   | Part One – To Begin With... | |
| 1 | Finding a Foundation | 11 |
| 2 | How Witches Work | 18 |
| 3 | Flavors of Witchcraft | 30 |
| 4 | The Journey Begins | 35 |
| 5 | Divination | 50 |
| 6 | Magick | 56 |
|   | Plants & Herb Appendix | 62 |
|   | Stone Appendix | 70 |
|   | Color Appendix | 74 |
|   | Part Two – A Peek at my Grimoire | 76 |
|   | Part Three – Recommended Reading | 110 |

# It's Witchcraft: A Beginner's Guide to Secular and Non-Secular Witchcraft

Jamie Weaver

Copyright © 2015 Jamie Weaver

All rights reserved.

ISBN: 9781098943875

# INTRODUCTION

Seventeen years ago, I became interested in witchcraft. I can't remember what drew me to it, but I do remember finding it fascinating, exciting, and mysterious. Even now, today, I still feel that way about witchcraft. After walking this path for seventeen years, I feel it's time to put my own knowledge and experiences out there in hopes of helping someone else along their own path. I don't have a degree in comparative religions or mythology, in fact, I have a bachelor's in criminal justice. I don't own my own occult shop, although I did try to keep up an online one for awhile. Throughout the work week I am an office assistant. I don't speak at gatherings or workshops, I don't even belong to a coven. So why on earth am I writing a book about witchcraft?

I've been reading about and researching witchcraft since I was about eight or nine years old. It's always called to me, it's something like coming home. Ever since I was little, I've practiced my own form of witchcraft (much of it made up when I was a little girl). On my eleventh birthday, I bought a tarot kit and taught myself how to read tarot cards. The tarot has helped me out of a lot of sticky situations and has even earned me some extra cash in college. During my first year of high school, I found Wicca. For the longest time, Wicca was my path. I loved it very, very much. I found a high priestess who I worked with (Hi Auntie M!), and she was a beautiful, strong woman who helped me along my Wiccan path for a long time.

Some of my friends were also interested in Wicca and so we did rituals together and spells too sometimes (especially for those loud upstairs neighbors at college). But once I graduated college, I felt my faith in Wicca shaking a little. Something was missing. It just wasn't sitting right with me anymore. It wasn't until just a few years ago, when I moved across the country, that I realized that Wicca wasn't for me anymore. I looked into working with Welsh deities, as that is part of my ancestry, but that wasn't sitting well with me either. Then, with the urging of my wonderful boyfriend (Hi babe!), I realized that it was time for me to make my own path.

So, as you can see, I am not a motivational speaker, nor a successful occult store owner, nor am I formally educated in world religions and mythology. I am just another witch, just like you. This book is my way of sharing my knowledge and my experiences, my way to lend a helping hand. I could go on about my own journey, but that's only part of this book, the rest of it is a way to help you along your own path.

You will find a lot of helpful information in this book as well as spells, meditations, divination techniques, and more. This book is meant to be a guide, a sign post along your path. It is by no means the end all be all of witchcraft. Take what you will from this book, let it help you on your way to the next sign post.

So...let's get started! First I'd like to address terminology and beliefs. I can't address every belief out there, but I will do my best to hit the main points. If you're looking for something more specific, you can always go to a local bookstore or library and see what they have or what they can order in for you. As for terminology, there unfortunately isn't one general consensus on terms when it comes to witchcraft. You will easily find five different definitions of an amulet if you look in five different books. Because of this, I will be as clear as I can, explaining how I see these things. If you agree with them, then feel free to run with it. If you find you like someone else's definition of what an amulet is, then run with that, but don't let that turn you away from the rest of the book. There may be a lot of things in here you haven't come across or thought of before.

Before you begin on this path, even just in reading this book, I have one suggestion. Leave all expectations behind. Expectations lead to hindrance. They will hold you back, limit you, and may very well discourage you. It's hard to think of witchcraft and not think of Charmed, The Secret Circle, Harry Potter, and even the more recently American Horror Story: Coven. It would be freaking awesome if witchcraft were really like that, but it's not. You may meditate two hundred and sixty four times before you feel absolutely centered and grounded or it may only take you three times, and that's okay.

To expect yourself to have instant results is unrealistic. It's even more unrealistic, and harsh, to become frustrated with yourself when you don't get instant results. Be patient with yourself and your craft, it will all come to you in good time. Even after you've had a moving experience, don't expect it to happen again the next time. It's good to go in blind each time, that way you're more open to whatever experience comes to you. By focusing on one experience you hope to get, you could easily miss a completely different one. It can be difficult to cast expectations to the side, but once you do, it makes things a lot easier and then you're not as hard on yourself.

With this book, as well as your path, be sure to take things at your own pace. There's no rush. If you want to move quickly from one thing to the next and you learn well that way, then do it that way. If you like to take things one step at a time and then take the time to let it all sink in and simmer, then do it that way. Everyone has their own experiences and everyone learns in their own way.

The witch's path is a beautiful and mysterious one. It can take you to many places, inside of you and outside of you. This is a path that helps you to learn and grow as a person. It is a path that has no end, you will always be learning, changing, evolving. That being said, don't let this be the only or the last book that you read. Keep reading, keep exploring, researching. And with that, welcome to the witch's path, I hope that you find everything that you're looking for.

**Note: Any recommended books, authors, or websites are resources that I have found helpful. I am in no way asking for compensation or recognition from said authors/creators.

## A Note From the Author

Some of you may be wondering, "Why a second edition? What's changed?" I've decided to release a second edition of *It's Witchcraft* and make the first edition unavailable for two reasons. One reason is simply to polish it up a bit by fixing some small grammatical errors and such. The main reason, however, is because I made a mistake in the first edition when explaining cultural exchange and cultural appropriation.

First off, let me explain what each of these words mean as they can be found in most dictionaries. Cultural appropriation is when practices, beliefs, activities, concepts, and customs are taken from another culture other than your own and used inappropriately with little or no acknowledgment of the culture it was taken from. This is often done by those of a more dominant culture. Cultural exchange or sharing, however, is when practices, beliefs, activities, concepts, and customs are mutually shared between two cultures. In this sense, there is reciprocity and understanding rather than just a one sided taking.

In the first edition of *It's Witchcraft*, I had a lapse of memory and mixed the two together. In the first edition, I stated that cultural appropriation could be bad, but wasn't always so long as nothing was taken or used unfairly, that this was how cultures learned from each other. This was incorrect. This was wholly my mix up and in doing so, I spread misinformation about cultural appropriation.

It's important that we know the difference between these two terms and not just in their definition, but also how they affect other people and cultures. Cultural appropriation takes without asking, it's selfish and hurtful, which can leave people and cultures that aren't a part of the majority feeling, once more, used and unimportant. No one should feel like this. So, instead of stepping toward cultural appropriation, let's instead move toward cultural sharing.

Cultural sharing or exchange has a much different affect than cultural appropriation in that it's a way of opening a door between people and cultures. Through this door we can work to understand one another and appreciate each other's differences. It's a two way street. Let's work together and learn from each other instead of taking what we want or what we think we want. Open a line of communication with someone, listen to them, hear them, understand their perspectives and their concerns, respect their wishes. We can only move forward if we work together.

I am very sorry if my mistake regarding these definitions has hurt or offended anyone. The last thing I want to do is hurt someone. My goal has always been to help people, but with this mistake there is a possibility that I have done the exact opposite. For that, I am very sorry. This is why I have discontinued the first edition of *It's Witchcraft* and included this explanation of the importance behind cultural sharing as well as the harm that comes from cultural appropriation.

Thank you for reading everyone, I hope you enjoy the second edition of *It's Witchcraft*.

# Part One – To Begin With...

## 1 Finding a Foundation

**What is witchcraft?**

Is it old hags with warts riding broomsticks? Is it busty blondes in black lingerie riding broomsticks? Is it cursing your neighbors? Bewitching your boss? Frogs tongues and fingernail clippings? Is it loving nature and worshiping a mother goddess? For many people witchcraft contains different things, focuses on specific beliefs, holds different values. Above all, witchcraft is just that – a craft. Witchcraft isn't tied to any specific religion or type of person.

Witchcraft can be used along side a religion or spiritual belief, but it's not required. Most often, we see witchcraft coupled with Wicca, an earth based religion that recognizes a father god and a mother goddess. Many Wiccans are witches, but not all witches are Wiccans. Because witchcraft is a craft, that means that it doesn't need religious belief. You can believe in no god at all and still use witchcraft effectively, you can still be a witch. This also means that you can couple witchcraft with your religious practice. So yes, this means that you can be a Jewish witch, a Christian, Muslim, or Pagan witch. Anyone can be a witch.

No one is naturally more capable of working witchcraft than anyone else. As I said before, anyone can be a witch. No matter your sex, gender, religious belief, age, physical state, mental state, sexual orientation, no matter who you are or how you identify yourself, you can be a witch if you want to be. That's all it takes, intent and action. As long as you want to be a witch and you do your best to work with witchcraft, then you're a witch. It's really that easy.

So, we know that anyone can be a witch, but what *is* witchcraft? Many people will give you different answers, but in a general matter it's fairly simple. Witchcraft is a craft in which you work with magick and energy, much in the same way an artist uses a paintbrush or a writer uses a pencil. With the use of tools such as herbs, stones, and other natural objects, a witch can work with energy to help produce their desired outcome. The process of manipulating energy in this way is called magick (spelled with a 'k' to differentiate from stage magic). There are many different ways to work magick, some of which will be explained later on in this book.

Put very simply: Witchcraft is a craft in which you use magick through natural objects and elements for your own means.

Yeah, but it's the devil's work, right? Wrong. The concept of Satan or the devil, is a religious concept, there is no religion in witchcraft unless you decide to use it that way. Witchcraft is not inherently evil or bad, but it's not inherently good either. Witchcraft is neutral, it's as good or evil as electricity. If you've ever seen the movie The Craft, they explain it perfectly, "True magic is neither black, nor white – it's both because nature is both. Loving and cruel, all at the same time. The only good or bad is in the heart of the witch. Life keeps a balance on its own." - The Craft, 1996.

Many believe that whatever creative force that runs through our universe, our world, and our very lives is neutral, like electricity. It's up to you if it should be used for good or bad purposes. So, then, what's good and what's bad? Sometimes it's simple: to use magick to curse a girl's partner and chase him away so that you can have her would be bad. But what if you use magick at her request to banish him from her life, because he's abusive towards her? That would be much more of the good. And sometimes, it's not so simple: someone who has hurt you is found not guilty in court, is it good or bad to curse them? Do you feel that disturbs the balance? That's up to you. In such personal, painful situations such as this, you may be the only one who can truly judge that.

Casting spells for other people can also be a tricky thing to figure out. Some believe that it's not right to cast spells on other people without their permission. Other people believe that it's bad to cast spells that mess with free will. So should you cast a healing spell on your elderly grandmother who just got out of the hospital without telling her? Your intentions are good, but is it right? That's up to you to decide.

Some witches believe that you should harm none, this includes casting spells for people without their permission and casting spells that mess with free will. The harm none belief is a widely known Wiccan tenet and is not held by all witches. It's definitely something to chew on though. How you draw your lines between right and wrong is tricky sometimes – this is one of those situations that you should take some time to think about it in relation to your own morals and values.

So how about getting your ex back? Or getting that new co-worker to go out with you? If you're casting a love spell on someone specifically with the intent of getting them to love you, you're messing with their free will. This is one of those times where I've got to put up my big old stop sign and there are a couple of reasons why. Messing with someone's free will is a pretty crappy thing to do to someone. How would you feel if someone you didn't like cast a spell on you to love them and lust after them? It's pretty much a magick roofie – not good, in any way, shape, or form. Besides, do you really want a relationship based on lies and manipulation? But don't fret, there are good, friendly love spells that can help you out without manipulating someone's free will, but we'll get to that later.

In a nutshell, this book will give you the basics of witchcraft in a non-religious capacity. But feel free to work what you learn here into your religious practice if that's what you want to do.

### *What is Magick?*

As mentioned above, magick is the manipulation of energy by using your intent, your own energy, and the energy of natural objects and the elements in order to create a desired outcome. Magick is working with energy, the energy that flows through everyone and everything. The world, our universe, is built on energy – as one of my high school science teacher's used to say, it's all physics, and in a way it really is. Everything and everyone is connected in a web of energy.

We affect that web everyday in everything thing we do, sending out ripples. With every action, we set something into motion, an irreversible change. Magick sends the energy of our intent along that web to set the right things into motion so that our desired outcome can come into being. Magick isn't making a pile of money poof onto your kitchen table, magick is creating the right circumstances for a new job opportunity or a promotion at work to occur.

There is energy in everything, but there's also a specific energy to things too. This is why you need specific objects for specific spells. For example: Rose quartz is used primarily for love spells, that's the type of energy that it vibrates, so you don't want to use it for money spells or protection spells. This is why it's important to know which uses certain stones, colors, herbs, and plants have. By using the correct ingredients, the chances of your spell being successful are greater.

There have even been new theories developed in the field of science to explain magick. Because magick is all energy work, energy moved and manipulated on different wave lengths, some scientists believe that evidence of magick can be captured by certain types of cameras that see on different light waves. But just because science can't explain something (right now or maybe ever), doesn't mean it doesn't exist. There are so many things about our own planet that we still don't know yet, we're still finding new creatures at the bottom of the ocean, new species of animals in our rain forests. Just because we don't know about it yet, can't prove it yet, doesn't mean it doesn't exist.

So, how do you use magick? Well, there are many different ways and many different ingredients and tools. But it doesn't matter how many herbs you've gathered or how many stones you've collected, it doesn't matter what types of tools you've bought or made; the most important ingredient and tool that you can ever have is your intent. Intent is key. Without it, your spells will go awry and possibly even backfire (never fun).

When your intent is shaky, when you're not sure of what you want or if it's the right thing to do, the stability of your spell is shifted, it's shaky. Be sure of what you're doing and why you're doing it. When your intent is sure and strong, your spell will be the same. All of the other tools you use will help to enhance your energy to guide your intent along the web of energy and set things in motion for your desired outcome, your *intended* outcome.

While intent is the most important aspect of working magick, it's not the only one. There are other factors to take into consideration. Energy doesn't just come from our own planet, but movement throughout our whole solar system as well. Our moon and planets also play a role in magick. Certain spells are best done during certain phases of the moon, other spells fare better when the moon is in alignment with certain astrological signs. There are also spells that benefit when cast during planetary alignments or when astrological signs are aligned with certain planets. This will also be explained later.

There are multiple things to take into account when working magick, and it can seem overwhelming at times, but don't be discouraged. It takes time to learn it. It may seem overwhelming now, but take it step by step, take your time, and you'll do fine.

### *How old is witchcraft?*

This is actually a hot topic of debate. Some people believe that witchcraft is an ancient path, stemming back long before Christianity. Others believe that it is a relatively more new (new as in the past fifty to one hundred years) craft that is becoming widely popular all over the world. There are also those who land in the middle, believing that there may have been something *like* witchcraft way back when, but that it was not like it is today. These are not the only views, but these are some of the widely known stances on the subject.

The truth is, no one really knows for sure. It's possible that something like witchcraft was practiced hundreds and thousands of years ago, but it's doubtful that it was what is practiced today. While this is an interesting topic of discussion, it's not something to get hung up on. Whether your path is old or new, all that matters is that it works for you and you're happy and comfortable with it. Everything was new once, give it time to grow and set it's roots before you judge it too harshly.

You may be wondering now about the witch hunts in Europe and New England. Some people refer to the time period of the witch hunts as "The Burning Times", the time when witches were tortured and killed for their craft. Some people see those who died in the witch hunts as martyrs, suffering in the fight so that we can practice freely today. This idea is very, very unlikely. The period of the witch hunts was a chaotic time, men and women were accused left and right of witchcraft.

Many of those accused were Christians, they just happened to make the wrong person angry. The disabled, the mentally ill, and feuding community members were usually those who were singled out as witches. It was a horrible time in history, no doubt, but these people were not martyrs for any cause. They were caught in the crossfire of fear, anger, and power struggle. Is it possible that some of them did practice some form of witchcraft or folk magick? Yes, it's possible, but we'll never know for sure.

### *Your Own Foundation*

So where do you stand in all of this? Before embarking on the witch's path, it's good to know where you stand, to know what your beliefs are, and what it is you're looking for. Do your own beliefs and values match with that of witchcraft. While witchcraft doesn't have any religious tenets, it does have it's own beliefs and basic structure. Witchcraft is a craft that works closely with nature. Now, this doesn't mean you have to go outside and hug a tree, but you can if you want.

Witchcraft works with five elements: Earth, Air, Fire, Water, and Spirit. Working together, these five elements create a balance, a strong foundation upon which to build. If you look at a pentacle, you see a five pointed star within a circle. Each point represents one of the five elements. Each element is connected within the star and by the circle wrapping them all together. This symbol shows the five elements connected to each other, all effecting each other, all being a part of each other, much like the web of energy that we live in and work with.

These five elements help create a balance and balance is very important to many witches. You can't have light without darkness and you can't have darkness without light. There is no life if there is no death and there is no give if there is no take. As mentioned before in the movie quote, nature keeps a balance of it's own. It's wise for us to live the same, keeping our own balance in whatever way that we can and know how.

This may be a good time for you to sit down and figure out where you stand and where your foundation is. You may need to ask yourself some questions before you move forward. Questions such as:

What am I looking for with witchcraft?

What is it that I want to achieve or gain?

What sort of doubts do I have and why?

What has drawn me to learn more about witchcraft?

Where do I draw the line in the sand between good and bad?

How do I feel about casting spells on others?

Do I want to use witchcraft with a religious practice?

Do I want to use witchcraft as just a craft?

It's good to know yourself, to know where you stand. Once you've answered these questions honestly, if you still want to walk the witch's path, then keep going. You may find that your answers to these questions will change over time. That's okay, we're human, we're constantly changing and evolving, it's normal, natural. When you've got your foundation and you're ready to practice witchcraft, it's time to start the journey.

But before you start walking, you should first start within. I've found it very helpful to start by building your altar within. What does this mean? This means starting with nothing but yourself. Once you've established your own inner sacred space, it's easier to do it physically. Plus, this way, if you're ever in a bind, you can reach within and have everything you need. To build an altar within, sit down in a quiet place where you'll be undisturbed.

Without the help of incense or candles, try to quiet your mind and center yourself as best you can. There are no expectations here, you don't have to empty your mind of every single thing. If something crosses your mind, that's okay, just focus on your breathing. Feel your body change as you take air in and let it out. This can be hard for some people, but just do the best you can, focus as much of your attention as you can on your breathing.

Once your mind is as quiet as you can get it, breathe deep a few times. This quiet, centered place in your mind and body is your inner altar. You can access it whenever you want. From this inner altar you can focus and direct your energy towards certain goals, you can meditate further to ground yourself or find answers from your subconscious, or you can just sit there at your inner altar and relax, just being there in that moment.

Do this a few times in a quiet place without interruptions. Once you've done it a few times there, do it at work during a break or at school during study hall. It's trickier to do with distractions, but the more you do it, the easier it will become over time. This is an altar that you can carry with you at all times, wherever you go. From here you will build upon your practice, this is your foundation.

## 2 How Witches work

### *By the Moon and Stars*

As previously mentioned, one of the ways many witches do their spell casting involves knowing the phases of the moon, the position of the astrological signs, and the movement of the planets. Each planet holds it's own qualities, as does the moon, and the astrological signs. So, if you're casting a spell for bravery, are you going to choose a night to cast your courage spell when your astrological sign is aligned with Mars or when it's aligned with Venus? There is an important difference here as Mars is known as the God of War and Venus is known as the Goddess of Love and Beauty.

Have you ever heard of Mercury in retrograde? This is when it appears as though Mercury is moving backwards. When Mercury goes into retrograde, this is an unlucky time for communication and making big decisions.. This is not a time to gamble, start new relationships, or start a debate. When Mercury is in retrograde, avoid risk taking. That being said, this is not the best time for spells, especially spells for love, luck, success, and justice. That doesn't mean you can't cast any spells when Mercury is in retrograde, it just means be careful. If you're going to cast any spells during this time, it would be wise to keep it to banishing spells, spells for ending relationships, and spells to stop bad habits.

There are many resources for finding out when a planet is where and when they enter astrological signs. Tarot.com is an excellent resource for finding this information. Annual witch's almanacs also tend to track when the moon is in which sign and which phase it's in when it's there. Below is a list of the planets and their attributes.

Mercury: Study, travel, logic, truth seeking, critical thinking, analytic, duality, communication.

Venus: Love of others, love of self, beauty, relationships.

Mars: Courage, war, strength, fortitude.

Jupiter: Money, growth, physical well being, prosperity, leadership, generosity, humanity.

Saturn: Limitations, caution, longevity, endings, cleansing, restraint.

Uranus: Intuition, awakening, new ideas, independence, outside the box thinking.

Neptune: Inspiration, compassion, imagination, emotions, sacrifice, clairvoyance.

Pluto (it is *so* a planet): Cooperation, regeneration, rebirth, change.

Our own moon is another great source of energy. The moon is linked to our world directly. It moves our oceans, times women's menstrual cycles, effects plants and animals. It is a beautiful light source and it too has it's cycles. The moon's four cycles are important to keep track of. If you don't track the planets and use that to your advantage, then you should definitely think about keeping track of the moon and using that information to time your spells. When the moon is full, this is a great time for spells involving love, lust, success, happiness, beauty, anything you want to become strong and bright. This is also a good time to gather herbs, because they too soak up the moon's light.

When the moon is shrinking, or waning, this is a good time for banishing spells, heartbreak management spells, ending relationships, coping with death, and spells to stop bad habits. Because this is a time of shrinking light, it's a good time to cast spells involved in weaning things out, beginning the process of ending. When the moon is dark and new, this is a good time for spells involving ending, cleansing, banishing, new projects, rebirth, and regeneration. As the moon grows brighter in it's waxing phase, this is a good time to cast spells for growth, love, fertility, lust, new relationships, healing, friendship, opportunities, luck, and anything else you want to expand, grow, or become stronger.

When the moon is in your sign, depending on the phase, this would be a good time to cast spells for personal growth, accessing your psychic abilities, and wish spells. Because the moon is linked with women's menstrual cycles, it is also a good celestial body to work with in terms of womanhood, menstrual cycles, menopause, and childbirth. If you are a female witch that experiences your menstrual cycles, you may want to consider keeping track of you cycle along side the phases of the moon. Some Native tribes would separate their menstruating women from the rest of the tribe, because they believed that during this time, women were closer to the gods and were more susceptible to visions. Given that, you may want to try isolating yourself for an hour or two during your menstrual cycle and meditate to see if you are able to tap into any sort of second sight or other psychic experiences.

### *Tools of the Trade*

Witches work with many different tools, but they don't all work with the same tools. Here I will give you an overview of some of the widely known and used tools that witches keep. You don't have to have all of these tools and you don't have to spend a fortune on them. As long as you have your inner altar, you have everything you need to work magick. These tools are just that, helpful tools that make it easier to concentrate on what you're doing and get you into a magickal, centered mindset more quickly.

In your research, you will find that other religions and spiritual paths use similar or even the same tools, but that doesn't mean that you have to use them in a religious aspect. Tools are tools. Your grandfather's crucifix necklace can be used as a religious item or it can be used as a symbol of protection or you could use it as a makeshift screw driver to unscrew something (although I find dimes and pocket knives work best for that).

Keep in mind that it's good to use your magick tools only for magick. If you often use your magick tools for mundane purposes, their energy wears off quickly. You may want to consider cleansing your tools every few months, during a new moon, to keep their energies clear for their magickal purpose.

*Athame.* The athame is a ritual knife, used to direct energy much like a wand. The athame, however, is also used to cut energy and to sever ties. The athame is never used in violence, ever. It is for magickal use only. If you want a knife for protection, try the army navy store. Athames are helpful during rituals, when you need to leave the circle. The athame can cut a door in the energy of the circle you've created during your ritual in case you've forgotten something outside the circle (happens to me all too often). Some witches believe that the athame needs to be black or white handled, while others feel that as long as it's a ritual knife, cleansed and consecrated for that purpose, it should do just fine.

*Cauldron.* This is a classic witch's tool. You can use it for brewing potions, but it's much easier now to use a pot on the stove than a cast iron cauldron over an open fire. Cauldrons are great for a couple of different uses. You can fill them with water and flowers for spring rites and rituals, you can fill them with water to divine with, you can build fires inside of them (keep a jug of water handy), or you can put self-igniting charcoal inside of them to burn resin incense and herbs with. Cauldrons come in all types of sizes and materials, but the most popular, and most effective in my own opinion, is the classic cast iron cauldron (I have three of various sizes myself). Some people also believe that the cauldron is a symbol of a mother goddesses, of the earth, and so the cauldron can also be used as a holy object, if that's what you choose to do.

*Wand.* The wand is a director of energy. It helps you to focus your energy and direct it where you want it to go. As mentioned above, the athame can be used in the same way, but in reality you don't have to use either. Your hand, with two fingers pointed, will get the job done just the same. For some, however, the wand and athame are helpful in keeping their concentration on what it is they're doing. Wands tend to be made from natural wood, not the hard plastic wood lookalike, bones, and even whole crystals.

*Broom or Besom.* This is a ritual broom, not the one with cat hair and dust all over it in a corner of your kitchen. No, this broom is used for a more specific purpose. You still use the broom to sweep, but instead of sweeping dust and dirt, you're sweeping away negative and distracting energies from your work space or your sacred space. Some witches believe that you have to make your own besom, but there are plenty of beautiful, handcrafted ones for sale in many occult shops.

*Instruments – bells, tambourines, drums, and rattles.* These instruments are very helpful for witches (shamans too). These instruments can help to break up toxic energy in your aura, signal the beginning of a ritual or rite, induce trance, build energy to work with, or summon spirits to join you during your ritual work.

*Feathers and Bones.* Many witches use certain animals parts, such as feathers, bones, and teeth, to help them in their work. Most witches do not kill animals for the sole purpose of using their parts in magick, many witches find feathers and bones in nature. You can also buy these things or salvage them from animals that have already passed on. It may sound gross, but it's pretty helpful. Feathers are used for a great deal of purposes. Some people use them in protection spells, spells for independence and freedom, cleansing spells or rituals, and much more. Bones are also used in many ways. They can be used in different forms of divination, to call upon ancestors or other spirits, to honor the dead, and more.

*Stones, Crystals, and Gems.* These are used for all sorts of different things. A witch may keep handfuls of stones, for whatever type of spell they may need them for. Clear quartz crystals are good for enhancing and magnifying energy while bloodstone is great for healing. Each stone, crystal, and gem vibrate their own energy, that of which can be used in certain spells and rituals. You can find a list of stones and crystals in the Stone Appendix of this book.

*Incense.* Incense is great for helping the mind calm and center.

Some scents are good for meditation while others are good for cleansing. To find out what scents to use, check out the Herb Appendix of this book. Incense can come in a couple of different forms, such as cone incense, resin incense, and stick incense. Stick and cone incense can burn on their own, but resin incense needs to be burned in a fire or on a self-igniting charcoal block (which can also be found in most occult shops).

*Sea Shells.* These are great for invoking or representing the element of water. Some witches use shells for divination, much like casting runes or bones. Spells for love, emotion, and change sometimes call for sea shells, as sea shells hold the essence of the ocean. The ocean, like emotions, is deep, beautiful, deadly, and tumultuous. This is why emotions, love, and change, are represented by water.

*Candles.* Candles are used for more than black outs, setting the mood, and getting rid of unwelcome stench. Candles are used often in rituals, meditations, and spells. Fire is powerful, creative, and destructive. It gives us the warmth to live by, but let out of control and it will destroy, much like power. The colors of candles are very important, as colors, like everything else, vibrate specific energies. So be sure to use red candles for love and lust, pink for friendship, black for banishing and protection, and green for money. Check out the Color Appendix in this book to learn more about the attributes of different colors.

*Herbs, Oils, and Plants.* Essential oils are derived from herbs and other plants, therefore they hold the attributes of the plants that they're taken from. Herbs are used for every kind of spell you can think of. They vibrate specific energies, so like colors and stones, you want to be sure you're using the right ones for your spells. The Herb Appendix in this book can help you out with some herb and plant attributes.

*Book of Shadows.* This is a type of spiritual journal for many witches. It contains different spells, divination outcomes, experiences, and private thoughts. Not quite a spell book, a book of shadows (or book of light, book of mirrors, etc) is more personal, much like a diary or journal. The term book of shadows comes from the belief that it is wise for witches to hide their craft from others for safety and to protect their personal practice. There are many names used in place of Book of Shadows, use whatever you like.

*Grimoire.* This is more like a spell book. A grimoire is a compilation of spells, rituals, recipes, and information. It's not a personal journal, but more of an instructional book. This is something that you can keep for yourself during your journey and eventually pass on to the next generation, if that's what you choose to do. While you keep your information in your grimoire, you can record the outcomes in your book of shadows.

Most occult stores carry these items. These tools can range in price from 'not too bad' to 'hmm...do I want to pay my rent this month?'. What's great though, is that you don't have to buy all of these tools. You can buy many tools second hand or you can make them yourself. Many witches make their own brooms and wands, just by going for walks or hikes and finding the materials they need and then working with what they find. If you're skilled in making books, you can make your own book of shadows and grimoire. Today, there are some witches that keep their book of shadows and grimoire on their computer or tablet.

Goodwill is a great store to visit to find second hand items to use in your craft. They tend to have a lot of bottles, candles, and other items you can use. If you're on the west coast (in America) St. Vincent de Paul's sells bars of wax, recycled from old candles, this way you can make your own candles at home and infuse them with whatever herbs and oils you want. You can always find items to turn into tools at flea markets, estate sales, thrift stores, and even out in nature.

Tool substitution is always an option too. If you can't make or afford a wand or athame, you can always use your own hands. If you don't have a cauldron, but you do have a clay pot you made in a ceramics class, that will get the job done. Be sure to cleanse and consecrate your second hand tools before you use them, they're most likely still carrying energy from other shoppers and previous owners. That energy can clash with whatever work you're trying to do.

Remember: When you have an altar within and your intent is strong, you don't need other tools. The other tools help and can make things easier, but they're not necessary or mandatory.

### *Working with the Elements*

There has been some mention throughout this book about the elements, but you're probably wondering what 'the elements' means and how witches use them. As mentioned previously, witches work with five elements: Earth, Air, Fire, Water, and Spirit. While all of the elements are connected and balance each other, they also have their own attributes. Because of these different attributes and energies, different elements are used for different spells. Not only that, but many of the tools listed above represent one or more of the elements in themselves.

Some witches like to have at least one of each element present on their altar or during spell casting to ensure balance in all of their magick. Then there are some other witches that work mainly with one element, such as sea witches (more on sea witchcraft later). These witches find a natural calling to one of the elements, a sort of inexplicable bond or tie to that element. So, let's take a look at what types of energies and attributes each element has. Below these explanations you will find a list of the tools mentioned above and their elemental correspondences.

*Earth.* Earth represents materialistic desires, home life, grounding, logic, wealth, success, foundation, roots, and stability. Working with the earth in spells is good for finding solutions to problems, money magick, grounding yourself, and inner growth. In the tarot, the disks/pentacles represent earth. Astrological signs that are tied to the earth element are Virgo, Capricorn, and Taurus. The cardinal direction that represents earth is North.

*Air.* Air represents thinking, daydreaming, imagination, mental powers, ideas, independence, influence, communication, and whimsy. Working with air is very helpful in magick concerning decision making, opening your mind, inspiration, concentration, communicating with people, communicating with spirits, and finding your voice. The swords represent air in the tarot deck. Astrological signs tied to air are Libra, Aquarius, and Gemini. East is the cardinal direction that represents air.

*Fire.* Fire represents desire, passion, lust, power, creativity, anger, ego, opportunity, motivation, and energy. Fire is a good element to work with when casting spells to find a lover, to spice up your love life, to find some creativity, to find new opportunities, to make wishes, and even give yourself some more energy when you're feeling lethargic. In the tarot, the wands or staves represent fire. The fire signs in astrology are Leo, Aries, and Sagittarius. The cardinal direction of fire is the South.

*Water.* Water is the element of emotion, love, psychic abilities, the place between life and death, creation, destruction, chaos, calm, and indulgence. Use water in spells for love, managing heartbreak, ending relationships, beginning relationships, contacting the dead, and further developing your psychic abilities. The tarot cards represent water through the suit of cups. The water signs in astrology are Cancer, Pisces, and Scorpio. The cardinal direction of water is the West.

*Spirit.* The element of spirit is the one found in all of us. Some witches also attribute it to deities and/or spirits. Tapping into the spirit element is good for finding inner peace, connecting with nature, communicating with the divine, finding your inner strength, and opening yourself to the gods.

Tool Correspondences:

| Athame: Air   | Cauldron: Water/Spirit       | Wand: Air/Fire    |
| Stones: Earth | Quartz Crystal: Earth/Spirit | Incense: Air/Fire |
| Candles: Fire | Bell: Water/Spirit           | Shells: Water     |
| Feathers: Air | Herbs: Earth                 | Bones: Spirit     |

### *Circle*

I've been throwing some jargon around like circle, ritual, rites; so what is all that? A circle is the barrier you put up during ritual. Rituals are times when you celebrate the seasons, the cycles of the moon, and menstrual cycles (these are not the only rituals out there, but they are some of the biggies). Rites are those of rites of passage, such as initiations, recognizing a death, recognizing a birth, reaching puberty, reaching menopause; basically, it's all of those milestones that come once in a lifetime for a person.

A circle is the barrier you put up between your sacred space/altar and the rest of the world. This barrier helps to keep out negative and distracting energies as well as harmful or meddlesome spirits. While in a circle, your intent is to conduct your ritual, rite, or spell. Now, you don't always have to raise a circle to cast a spell, but some witches like to. Raising a circle is pretty simple and there are many different ways to do it. Basically, what you want to do is cleanse and consecrate the area and trace or set up a physical circle or points around the circle to show where that barrier is.

The usual sequence of raising a circle starts with cleansing an area, you can do this with a broom, smoke, a rattle, or a feather. Then you can consecrate the area, usually done by spoken word, smoke, salt water, or chant along with marking the circle. These are not the only ways to raise a circle, but it's some of the more well known procedures. The circle stays there while you do your work. Sometimes, you may find that you have to leave the circle. You may have to use the bathroom or retrieve something you've forgotten. That's what the athame is for.

The athame can cut a doorway in the circle. To cut a doorway, do so up, across, and down from right to left. When you're outside the circle, quickly close the doorway, by cutting back the opposite way, from left to right. When you come back to the circle, cut it open again, step through, and close it once more. It's not good to keep cutting doorways, it makes the energy shaky, so try your best to pee before circle and bringing everything you need in ahead of time. Because crossing the barrier can weaken or undo it, it's good to keep kids and pets away during your circles.

To take down a circle, there are a few things you can do. Just stepping over the boundary can do it, so can sweeping up any physical marker that you placed down (with a regular broom). You can also say that the circle is closed or that it is now undone. There are a few different ways to do it. Later on, in Part 2, I will give you the process of how I create and take down circles.

## *Working Skyclad*

Do witches really work naked? Some do yes, but not all. That's what working skyclad means, working naked. Some witches believe that working magick without the barrier of clothes gets you closer to nature, that it increases your bond with the earth, making your magick stronger. Is this true? Well, I've tried both, and to me it seems to be exactly the same, clothes or no clothes, so I prefer to work clothed, but that's just me.

While working skyclad may help you feel closer to nature and may help boost your magick, there are some things to consider. If you're working outside and are working skyclad, are you in a safe place? If you get caught, are you going to get into trouble? If you're working with other people, do you feel comfortable and safe being naked around them? While nudity is natural, it's frowned upon in our society depending on the context. It would probably put a bit of a damper on your circle if a cop fines you for public nudity. There are, unfortunately, people out there who are also predators. If you are practicing skyclad with others, be sure you know them well and trust them, personal boundaries can be a very good thing.

Working skyclad is one way of doing magick, but how about clothed. Some witches have specific clothes and even robes that they wear for working magick and holding rituals. These clothes tend to be worn only for magickal purposes and not day to day. Kind of easy to see how a casting dress can lose it's magickal energy and feel when you wear it to the grocery store. Some witches also wear ritual jewelry and even crowns during their rituals. These tend to be talismans or amulets.

Temporary tattoos, such as henna, can also be used for rituals and working magick. If you're casting a spell for fertility, it could help very much to use henna to draw fertility symbols on your body. You could even infuse the temporary tattoo with herbs or oils and wear it with you, a sort of spell that you carry with you on your body, similar to a charm.

What you choose to wear, or not to wear, for working magick and holding rituals is up to you. It all comes down to what you're comfortable with. If you find a local coven that practices skyclad and you're not comfortable with that, let them know. Maybe that's not the coven for you or maybe you can work something out with them so that you don't have to be naked during the ritual or rite (as long as you don't mind others being naked that is). If you're not comfortable with working naked, you don't have to and no one can make you. It's your choice.

## *Working with Spirits and Ancestors*

Some witches work directly with spirits and sometimes the spirits of their ancestors. These spirits could be spirits of the dead, spirits of the earth, guardian spirits, or divine spirits much like the Lwa in Vodou. Witches who work with the spirits, be they ancestral or otherwise, tend to have shrines for those spirits. A shrine is different from an altar in that an altar is a work space for magick, while a shrine is a way to honor a spirit or a god/goddess.

Working with spirits can be tricky, but also helpful. Some spirits are tricksters while some are stubborn and others are helpful and friendly. Spirits hold many of the same emotions that we do, so it can sometimes be difficult to work with a spirit if they're feeling stubborn or temperamental. This is where offerings and giving thanks helps a lot, along with being understanding of the spirits. They have more to do than just sit around and wait for you to call, so patience is definitely a virtue.

Be sure to give thanks and leave offerings for the spirits. Some spirits like specific items. For instance, in Vodou, Papa Gede enjoys coffee and dark colored sweet drinks like soda, so if you asked him for a favor, it would be helpful and respectful, to leave him a bit of coffee, maybe with a shot of rum too. If you're working with ancestors, it always helps to have items of theirs or images of them on your shrine or altar. If you knew that ancestor personally, it would also be good to have an offering for them that you know they would like. When working with spirits, always be careful, be sure you know who or what you're calling upon.

### *Working with Deities*

As mentioned before, witchcraft can be worked into religion if you choose to do so. Some witches work with deities, gods, and goddesses. Some witches have patron deities in which they work closely with that god or goddess, similar to working with spirits. There are witches who choose to work with certain deities and then there are those who find certain deities choosing them. Some witches have dreams in which deities reach out to them or they see the deity during a trance, from that moment some witches will agree to work with that deity.

If you do choose to work with a deity, do your research first. The mythology behind a god or goddess can give you some good insight on what type of deity they are and how you can worship them. If you decide to work with a deity from a culture that is not your own, be careful. Some cultures are closed to outsiders and to take from that culture is disrespectful and downright rude. As mentioned in my author's note at the beginning of this edition, taking from a culture without due respect, recognition, and often some sort of understanding or permission (especially if it's a closed culture or religion), this is cultural appropriation. Such behavior is damaging, hurtful, and disrespectful to cultures and people's own identities.

Cultural sharing or exchange, however, is much more fair and respectful. This is the equal and honest sharing of ideas and customs from one culture to another. Unlike cultural appropriation, cultural sharing is *give and* take. This type of sharing and exchange can help us understand each other's feelings and perspectives while also helping us teach each other interesting things about ourselves. It gives people the opportunity to say, "No, you shouldn't use that, because it's sacred to my people and our practice of this." and then you can brainstorm to find something else you can do. We can't just take and we can't just talk, we also have to give, listen, and understand.

It's always good to broaden your knowledge, to learn about different cultures, this is just one way that we learn and grow as human beings, so long as you're not hurting people or disrespect them and their culture in the process. So before choosing a deity from another culture, do some research, find out if that culture is closed to outsiders or not.

When working with deities, it's wise to also give thanks and leave an offering for them. Referencing back to mythology can help you find what sort of offerings deities enjoy.

### *Divination*

Divination is another tool that witches often use. Divination is the art of of using specific items or tools to tell the past, present, and future. Often times it's referred to as fortune-telling, but this is incorrect. Divination tells of fortune, misfortune, answers questions, explains situations in further detail, and much more. What's great about most divination is that it explains your current situation, what you've done in the past, and where you're headed if you continue to do things the way you have been thus far, but you're always able to change the course of your actions and come to a different outcome than originally foretold.

There are many different ways to divine. One of the most popular is reading tarot cards. This consists of a 78 card deck. By placing the cards down in specific spreads you can find answers to questions and learn more about current situations. Runes work similarly to tarot cards in that you lay them out in a spread, but more than placing them, you throw them. Many rune readers carry squares or circles of cloth with designs painted or drawn on them. Depending on where certain runes fall, you can read them much like you can read tarot cards.

Tea leaves are similar to runes and tarot cards, but they can be trickier to read sometimes. Depending on how the tea leaves rest in the tea cup and what forms and shapes they take, you can read them. Just as with tarot cards and runes, you can ask a specific questions or you can have a general reading done. In some cultures, coffee grounds are used instead of tea leaves, but the same process is used for the most part.

Pendulums are also helpful tools and they help with specific yes-no questions and answers. Pendulums are stones, crystals, or sometimes even just something as simple as an old key on the end of a chain or string. By holding the pendulum in one hand, you can ask the pendulum if left to right or forward and back is yes and which is no. From there you can ask questions and find their answers. I've had mostly positive results with pendulums. I used a pendulum to find out the exact date my second nephew would be born and it was correct.

Spirit boards and Ouija boards are another form of divination as well as a way to communicate with spirits. These tools tend to get a bad reputation, but as long as you are careful with them and are respectful, you shouldn't have a problem. I've also used Ouija boards, but haven't had a lot of foretold events actually occur. But that could be due to who I used to board with rather than it wasn't working well (honestly, most of my Ouija use happened in middle and high school, so you tell me how trustworthy girls at slumber parties are when it comes to Ouija boards).

Dreams can also be used for divination, but it doesn't usually happen easily or often. When I was in grade school I had two dreams that came true, with frightening detail. But since I've grown older, I've had fewer prophetic dreams and much more far apart. But it doesn't always have to be a prophetic dream, sometimes certain symbols in dreams can foretell something that's to come. If you're interested in interpreting dreams, I suggest finding a good dream dictionary.

This is all just a brief summation of some popular forms of divination. If you're interested in learning more about divination, keep reading. There's a chapter set aside just for divination later on.

# 3 Flavors of Witchcraft

There are many different types of witchcraft. It is a very flexible craft, one that can be tailored to suit most witches' wants and needs. As explained before, you don't have to do anything you're not comfortable with, you don't have to use the same tools as the witch next to you, and you can work it into your religion if you follow one. There's more to witchcraft's flexibility and creativity though. It's a craft that you can work into your everyday life, a craft that you can work to focus on your hobbies or lifestyle.

This chapter contains some of the more well known types of witchcraft. These are not the only types of witchcraft though. As you continue down your path I'm sure you'll find many more different forms of witchcraft. Each type of witchcraft has it's own unique flair. One type may work better for one witch than another, simply because of who they are, what their life is like, and what sort of values and interests they hold.

Keep an open mind as you read through these flavors of witchcraft, you may find something that really speaks to you. If none of these sound good to you, that's okay too, you can always create your own path or continue your search for what it is that you're looking for. Also keep in mind, that not everyone's craft, just like not every person, fits into a box or label. Some people practice their practice and don't care to title it, that's fine too. Each practice is personal to each witch, their path is their own just as yours is your own. As with other aspects of life, try not to label someone's craft if they don't choose to label it, that's just how they practice and it's their business.

### *Kitchen Witchcraft*

A kitchen witch works just like any other witch, but they focus more of their practice, as you can guess, in the kitchen. Kitchen witchcraft uses many of the same tools as other types of witchcraft, but it also incorporates food and drink. Kitchen witches will actually cook spells into their food, using special cooking tools that are just for their craft. This type of witchcraft can be very helpful when your family all crowds into your tiny apartment and Uncle Richie has refused to talk to Aunt Shelly in years and now they have to sit next to each other. All it could take is some lavender bread baked with a peaceful, harmonizing intent to smooth over the sour moods.

Kitchen witches try to have their altars in their kitchens, as the kitchen is their work space. Kitchen witches tend to be very mindful of their ingredients, in a magickal aspect as well as a nutritional aspect. Each ingredient can be very specific for some kitchen witches, so it's good to use both instinct, culinary knowledge, as well as magickal knowledge when practicing kitchen witchcraft. Many kitchen witches also worship hearth goddesses, but as always, this is up to you to decide if you want to practice this way.

### *Sea Witchcraft*

A sea witch is sometimes referred to as a water witch. Water, especially the ocean, represents the place between worlds, love, change, creation, destruction, calm, chaos, psychic ability, and emotion. The sea has a great deal of energy as well as a beautiful, charming allure, so it's no surprise that many witches are drawn to it. Sea witchcraft uses a lot of natural items from the sea, items such as sand, shells, water, seaweed, coral, and more.

Some sea witches use sea shells for divination, much like casting runes. Because sea water is such a great tool for connecting with one's psychic ability, it is also good to use for divination in the same way a crystal ball would. Many sea witches use magick to work with the ocean for safe voyages across the water, weather working, and moon magick. Because of it's connection to the ocean, many sea witches also work closely with the moon. While some sea witches live near the sea, not all do. When an ocean is not available, many find that a lake or river will suffice, given that all water represents the same things listed above.

If you're interested, there are some great tales out there about sea witches. While not all have basis of fact, they are still interesting and fun to read.

### *Hedge Witchcraft*

Hedge Witchcraft has been often compared to shamanism and is sometimes referred to as a type of shamanism. Hedge witches work heavily with herbs for healing purposes, but not just for healing magick. One main practice that separates hedge witches from other witches is that they project themselves, traveling to the other side, to the spirit world. This is why hedge witchcraft is at times compared to shamanism as shamans are known to travel into ghost worlds, the afterlife, the astral plane, and other such places for purposes of healing and communing with spirits.

Because of their traveling to the other side, many frequently work with spirits. So, if you're interested in working with spirits and/or ancestors, hedge witchcraft might be something worth looking into. Hedge Witches often also follow an earth based spirituality of some kind, one that helps them connect with the earth similarly to how they connect with spirits.

### *Green Witchcraft*

Green witchcraft focuses heavily on nature. This includes working with natural items, connecting with the earth, and sharing and exchanging energy with the earth. Green witches are known as naturalists, healers, and herbalists. They work with nature, connecting and communing with it while also protecting the bond between nature and all of its creatures (human and animal alike). Green witchcraft focuses heavily on the knowledge of herbal uses, both magickal use and medicinal use.

Many green witches pull from folklore and use folk magick, but this isn't always the case. Some green witches also work with the Fey (also known as fairies – not like Tinkerbell) which are sometimes also seen as earth spirits.

### *Family Witchcraft*

When witchcraft first started becoming popular in the 1960's and 1970's, many people came out claiming that their own families had been secretly practicing witchcraft for generations. Many of these stories featured a wise old grandmother who taught the family craft to them. While nothing could ever be proved or disproved, many of these claims were not taken seriously. Witchcraft had just started becoming popular, almost mainstream at the time, so many people thought that these family crafts coming out of the woodwork seemed to be a bit too convenient.

Despite who was embellishing and who was telling the truth, the fact of the matter is that today there are some family witchcraft traditions out there. Now that more people have been practicing since the '60's and '70's and even as early as the '50's, it is more likely that there are family witchcraft traditions out there now.

*Crafting Your Own Craft*

If you find that these forms of witchcraft and some other forms you've found don't quite fit for you, there's always the option of forging your own path. Now, this isn't always easy and it can be quite tricky too. But once you've done it, you know that it fits just right for you. Later on in your life you can even share it with others, bringing others in, or passing it down through your family as a family witchcraft tradition.

If you do decide that you want to make your own craft path, there are a couple of things you want to consider. What do you want to achieve with your form of witchcraft? What sort of philosophies do you want to build into it? What's important to you in your life that you can weave into your craft? What values do you want to incorporate into your craft as guidelines and beliefs? These are just a few things to consider when creating your own path.

When building your own craft, you also want to consider what types of tools you want to use, how you want to raise and take down a circle, whether or not you'll celebrate the cycles of our world and bodies, what types of beings you want to work with if any, and how to stay centered. Be patient with yourself when making your own path, it's not easy. It takes a lot of trial and error, but if you want to do it and you do your best, then you're golden.

## *Respect and Understanding*

Even today, it's hard for many witches and all of the different forms of witchcraft to be recognized as actual craft and to be taken seriously by others. Along the path you may find that some people will think you're being silly or going through a phase. You may even get my personal favorite, "Like...what? All that Harry Potter stuff?" Yes. Like all that Harry Potter stuff. Many of my fellow Potter fans will agree with me when I say, "If only."

So because witches do come up against some bad mouthing and name calling, it makes it all the more important that we understand and respect each other. Now, I'm not saying to give all of your admiration and respect to someone simply because they're a witch, but to have a general respect for their right to practice the way that they want to. Fighting amongst ourselves will only spread negativity and bitterness, it's better to remain calm, communicate, and try to understand each other.

While you may not agree with one person's way of practicing witchcraft, that doesn't give you the right to belittle them or disrespect them for it just as no one else as the right to belittle you or disrespect you because they don't agree with the way that you practice. You don't have to agree with someone to understand them.

# 4 THE JOURNEY BEGINS

You've done some research, you may have even found which form of witchcraft you want to pursue, but what now? Now, the journey really begins. In this chapter we will be discussing the different types of rituals, rites, holidays, spells, daily practices, and other forms of magick that witches partake in. We will also get to covens, solitary work, and much more. Keep in mind that you don't have to practice all of these things or incorporate all that's listed here, but it's definitely something to chew on and consider.

### *Some R & R: Rites and Rituals*

Earlier, I touched briefly on rites and rituals. As mentioned before, rites are celebrations of the milestones that happen once in a person's life. We can celebrate and hold rites for ourselves and others. Rituals happen much more often than rites as they are seasonal, monthly, and sometimes weekly. Ritual celebrations are held during the Sabbats. Wait now, what's a Sabbat? A Sabbat is a seasonal holiday among many witches.

Many witches celebrate the change of seasons throughout the year, also called the turning of the wheel. There are 8 seasonal holidays that these witches celebrate and they are: Samhain (pronounced sow-in, rhymes with cow-in) on October 31st, Yule/the winter solstice celebrated on December 21st, Imbolc on or around February 2nd, Ostara/the spring equinox on March 21st, Beltane celebrated on May 1st, Midsummer/the summer solstice celebrated on June 21st, Lughnassadh (pronounced loo-nah-sah) on August 1st, and Mabon/the fall equinox which is celebrated on or around September 22nd.

Witches celebrate the Sabbats differently while some don't celebrate them at all. Witches that work very closely with nature revere each seasonal holiday as an important stepping stone on their journey through the year. Some witches that incorporate witchcraft into their religion celebrate the Sabbats as holy days while some other religious witches don't celebrate them, but rather their religion's holidays, and then there's those who celebrate both. So before we move on, let me briefly explain each Sabbat and its meaning.

*Samhain.* Also known as Halloween and The Witch's New Year, this is the end of the harvest season. This is when many gods/goddesses go into the underworld or wither away with the land. It's a time for celebration, preparation, and honoring. This is the time to celebrate all that has passed in the past year. It is also the time to prepare for the long winter months to come. This is the night when the veil between worlds is thin. Spirits are able to walk more easily among us now and it is believed that relatives even return home for a visit.

Samhain is a good time to play games, use divination, and honor our loved ones who have passed on. You may want to construct a shrine to your ancestors or put out a 'dumb supper' which is a meal for the dead. If you have access to your ancestor's graves you can also go there to leave offerings and tokens of thanks for them. Apple divinations are very popular at Samhain. One popular apple divination is to sit in a chair with a bucket or large bowl of water behind you. Carve a long strand of the apple's skin with a knife and then throw that strand over your shoulder into the water. It is said that the apple peeling will take the shape of the first initial of the person you are meant to marry.

This is a great time to try to communicate with the dead as well as work with spirits. Types of magick and spells to be done on this night are honoring spells for the dead, banishing spells, spells of ending, divination, healing, inner journeying, growth, knowledge, protection, and communication.

*Yule.* This holiday is revered as a time of turning back to light. It is the shortest day of the year, but from this point on, the days will grow longer. This is a time of hope, renewal, and regeneration. You may wish to build an altar or shrine for the sun. You may even want to say goodbye to the darkness and to show your thanks for the growth you've done since Samhain. Many witches will burn a yule log on this night to signify the growth of light and to welcome the sun.

Yule is a time for home and hearth magick. Because we try to stay in our homes and out of the cold, now is a good time to focus on the energy of your home and what you want to bring into it. This is also the time to begin daydreaming. Spring is coming and soon you'll sew the seed of new ideas and dreams. There is still rest to be had, but prepare for growth in the coming months.

*Imbolc.* Like Yule, this holiday is one of regeneration and hope. The sun is growing brighter and the days longer everyday. Because of this, witches light many candles to usher Imbolc in. At this time, many animals carry unborn babies in their bellies. Some witches revere this holiday as a celebration of the mother and the divine mother. With this in mind, those witches will keep their cauldrons center stage, so to speak, as the cauldron often represents the womb of the mother.

Hearth and home magick are good for this holiday, as are spells for creativity, drive, protection, beginnings, starting new projects, new love, new friendships, clear and logical thinking, growth, and fertility. One popular way to celebrate Imbolc is to plant some seeds of your choice in an indoor pot. Bury the seeds along with a small bit of paper that contains your new ideas, dreams, and hopes. Your intent will grow and flourish as the plant grows and flourishes.

*Ostara.* This Sabbat is well known for it's fertility. If ever you were to do a fertility spell it would be today. Gardeners and farmers are planting their seeds for the season and so should you. Now is the time to take the first step toward any goals you have. You don't have to rush into anything, but now is the time to take that first step. Much like Easter, Ostara is symbolized by eggs, rabbits, birth, and rebirth. This is the time when the earth is awake and starts to stretch itself upwards.

Ever popular is dyeing eggs around this time, and you can do so for Ostara too. One thing you can do to celebrate this Sabbat is to decorate hard boiled eggs with symbols of any intent you have for inner growth and development. For example, let's say that you may be self-conscious and you would like to strive to be more confident in yourself. You can write the word confidence on the egg and dye it an appropriate color (red or orange would work). When you're ready, take some time to meditate over the egg. Visualize yourself achieving your goal of a more comfortable, confident you. When you're done, peel the shell and eat the egg, visualizing all of that intent and energy soaking into you as you consume it.

Ostara is a time for magick involving love, friendship, growth, happiness, fertility, inner and outer beauty, and adding strength or energy to a goal. Continue taking steps toward your goal or goals that you decided on at Imbolc.

*Beltane.* Where Samhain was a time of celebrating death and those who have passed on, Beltane is the time to celebrate life. Like Ostara, Beltane is a good time for fertility, as the plants continue to grow higher and fuller. Many witches celebrate this holiday outside in the sunshine (and sometimes even when it's raining), to celebrate the life that is all around them. This is also a good time to look back and reflect on how much you've grown since Samhain, the plants aren't the only ones that continue to grow.

The first rain of May is a powerful one, be it on Beltane or somewhere in the middle of the month. When you see that it is raining for the first time in May, collect some rain water. Any brew, potion, or spell that you add this water to is amplified by the energy of this rain. The first time I collected May's first rain it was a hailstorm, quite a bit of energy in that water!

Beltane is a great time for many forms of magick. Spells for growth, love, lust, fertility, happiness, friendship, energy, motivation, inspiration, success, and strength would do good to be cast on Beltane.

*Midsummer.* The day stretches long on Midsummer, it's the longest day of the year. The fields and orchards are booming with the promise of an abundant harvest. This day is one of happiness, cheer, and giving thanks. We worked with the earth from the cold winter months up to this point, and now there is bounty everywhere you look. It's said that any herbs gathered on Midsummer are the most powerful and potent herbs of the whole year.

Now is a good time to gather with friends and family to laugh, dance, and celebrate with the last long light of summer. Be sure to give your thanks to the earth, any spirits or gods/goddesses you work with, and the people around you who have helped you throughout the year thus far. Spells that are good to cast on Midsummer are spells for luck, happiness, success, protection, thanks, culmination, peace, harmony, and abundance.

*Lughnassadh.* This Sabbat marks the beginning of the harvest. Grains are mostly harvested at this time and so, bread is often baked and shared on this day as well as ale, mead, wine, and beer. This is the first day of the preparation for winter, but the summer light and warmth is still with us. Enjoy the warm days while they last, but look forward to the rest that is to come as the air grows cooler and the nights longer. An older tradition that's practiced on Lughnassadh is the making of corn dollies or corn husk dolls.

With a bit of peaceful and protective intent, you can craft these corn husk dolls with herbs inside them. Use lavender for peace and sage or rosemary for protection. You can even make a corn husk doll for each person in your home with these spelled herbs inside to bring them peace and protection. Good spells to cast on Lughnassadh are spells for protection, abundance, home and hearth, friendship, peace, harmony, comfort, and luck.

*Mabon.* The harvest is in full swing now. The end of the year is on its way and there's still preparation to be done. The days are shorter and colder now, the promise of winter is ahead. While this may be disappointing or sad for some, it is also a time of rest and relaxation. The earth is moving towards a long sleep so that it can return in spring, ready to begin anew. Mabon is the witch's harvest festival, a time of thanksgiving. It is also the time of reflection.

Now is the time to look back on the past year, to look at our successes and failures and to see them as teachers, not things to brag endlessly about to others or to beat ourselves up about. Give thanks to your spirits, gods/goddesses, friends, family, the earth, and to yourself. Mabon is a time for spells of ending, receding, banishing, healing, protection, inner growth, reflection, thanks, and strength.

These are just some general blurbs about each Sabbat, but each witch celebrates a little bit differently and according to their religious path if they follow one. It's always good to go out and learn more, so if these Sabbats interest you, do some research on their history, mythology, and modern practice. Rituals are held on each of these Sabbats by those who celebrate them. These rituals usually have appropriately decorated altars (leaves and pumpkins for Samhain, fresh berries and flowers on Midsummer) and some sort of spell or activity to welcome the next step in the year or to work with the earth as it changes in its cycle.

There are also many witches who hold rituals during the different phases of the moon. Depending on the cycle, the altar is appropriately decorated (bowl full of water and jasmine for the full moon, black candles and cauldrons full of water for the new moon) and there may be a spell or activity done to honor that cycle. Some witches do similar rituals to honor menstrual cycles, be it their own or someone else's. You can find rituals for these cycles and holidays in part 2 of this book.

### *Practices to Help With Spellwork*

It can be hard to cast spells and participate in rituals when your brain won't quiet down or when it refuses to focus. When this happens, we can become easily distracted or doubtful of ourselves which hinders and confuses our energy and intent. Luckily, there are some things you can do regularly to help you quiet and focus your mind. By practicing these exercises frequently, you will find it easier over time to quiet and focus your mind. Listed below are some things that you can practice to help turn down the volume and enhance you focus.

*Meditation.* For some people, meditation is a hassle and is very hard to do. And for good reason. There are thousands of ways to meditate with a thousand more techniques. The stereotype, and the often held expectations of ourselves, is that when you meditate you're supposed to make your mind go completely blank, to "go zen". While this is possible, it is not easy and it takes many, many, many years of practice to be able to do this even for just a few minutes. So don't beat yourself up if you can't make your mind go completely blank, I did that for a long time and it only made me more doubtful and frustrated.

Then there are the hundreds of kinds of meditations ranging from simple breathing meditations to super detailed, guided meditations. But on top of that, there are all the different ways that people tell you how you should breathe when you meditate. If I breathed during meditation the way that everyone told me to, I would sound like an asthmatic elephant with the hiccups. Some say to breathe into your belly instead of your lungs, this way you get more breath into your body. Some say to breathe in, counting to three and breathe out counting to four, while others say in four and out five.

Half-way through you may find it's gotten complicated rather quickly and then find yourself wondering, why bother? For the longest time, meditation stressed me out because I didn't know how to do it with all of the different directions I was getting and I was afraid that I was doing it wrong. Meditation is not supposed to stress you out. So, I decided to throw away everything I'd been told about meditation, and revamped it in a way that worked for me and didn't stress me out.

The type of meditation I'm talking about is a lot simpler. The goal is only to quiet your mind, to only have some things pop up here and there instead of thoughts shooting around like rush hour traffic on the Driscoll Bridge on the Garden State Parkway on your way into New Jersey (which is terrifying in case you were wondering). We live in a very busy world, it's hard not to think a mile a minute, but meditation can help with that. If you also find yourself stressing out about how to breathe during meditation and what type of meditation to do, let me offer you one way I do it. And if you don't like that or any other way you find, you can always create your own.

This simpler way of meditating starts with breathing, normally. If you normally breath deep then do that, if you normally breath shallow, then do that. Just breath normally and focus on it as best you can. Feel how your body changes as you breathe, how your chest rises and falls, how any aches or pains stretch as you breathe, how your head and muscles feel. Do nothing but focus on that breath when it comes in and when it goes out, naturally.

Your mind will wander. That movie I watched last night had a weird plot. I forgot to pick up toilet paper at the store. Why won't my neighbor's dog shut up? I should eat that chicken tonight before it goes bad. This is normal, try not to get frustrated with yourself. When these thoughts come up, just refocus to your breathing. Do this until you feel you're done. Hopefully by the end of it you'll feel a bit more relaxed and clear headed, but if not, don't fret, it takes time.

For some people, a quiet place is not a happy place. Sometimes when we sit in quiet we can start to be haunted by our own ghosts. Those who have anxiety, depression, and PTSD might find that guided meditation and visualizations work better for them than quiet meditations. Guided meditations and visualizations help to quiet and focus the mind just as well as quiet meditations do. When our minds are quiet and focused, we are centered, and being centered means we are better able to work magick.

*Daily Devotions.* These are pretty quick and easy to do for the most part. A daily devotion is just that, a devotion you make everyday to your practice, gods/goddesses, spirits, or the earth itself. There are many pre-written daily devotions out there and many of them are beautifully constructed, but you can also create your own if you want to. Daily devotions project positive energy into your craft while also focusing your mind. They can be very helpful, but you have to be active in them. That means to really say the words, mean them, don't just vomit them back from the page or from memory.

By repeating your daily devotions like a tape player, you're not really putting your energy into it. Be sure that the devotion you do daily really speaks to you, that it really means something to you. Just like with spells, if there's no intent, it's just words. In part 2 of this book I have provided my own daily devotion that you can try out if you like.

*Visualizations.* These are similar to meditation in that they clear and focus your mind. Guided meditation incorporates visualization for clear focus of the mind. Visualization is when you clearly picture a scene in your mind. You put yourself there mentally, seeing, feeling, tasting, hearing, and touching whatever is in that scene.

Visualization is extremely helpful when working with magick. Your energy can be projected in a clearer and more direct way when you can visualize your intent as if it is right in front of you. Sometimes it's good, even after you've done a spell, to visualize your intent as you lay down and go to sleep at night to continue sending energy in that direction, towards that goal.

All of these exercises can help you to ground, focus, and center yourself. Part 2 of this book contains some helpful exercises that you can try out.

### *Starting at the Root: You*

It's very wise to start your journey on the witchcraft path by knowing yourself, to understand why you're doing this, what you wish to gain, but also to look into certain facts about yourself that you may not know yet. Earlier, we discussed the five elements and how four of those elements are tied to specific astrological signs. When working magick and working with divination, it is wise to know your sign. You may find it even more helpful toward your craft to know your full astrological chart. Tarot.com has a great astrological calculator to help you find out a good deal of this information.

Once you know your astrological sign, you know what element you are cosmically tied to. But not all witches focus on working with the element tied to their sign. For example, I'm a Virgo, with a Gemini rising sign, no water in there at all, yet I'm very drawn to water and I love working with it. Do you find yourself drawn to a specific element? One that you would enjoy working with frequently in your spellwork and rituals?

Depending on what your astrological sign is, you will also want to know which planet your sign is tied to. This information is good to have when you're doing magick and any time you are consulting the stars and planets. Below is a list of the astrological signs and their ruling planets:

Aries – Mars

Taurus – Venus

Gemini – Mercury

Cancer – The Moon

Leo – The Sun

Virgo – Mercury

Libra – Venus

Scorpio – Pluto

Sagittarius – Jupiter

Capricorn – Saturn

Aquarius – Uranus

Pisces – Neptune

Remember! You are your most important tool in your witchy toolbox, so it's good to know where your energies align and what influences them. This information can also come in handy for certain types of divination which we'll discuss later.

### The Broom Closet

The Broom Closet is a popular expression used in the witchcraft community for those who are not "out" about their craft. Everyone has their own personal reasons for being either in or out of the broom closet. Some people fear discrimination, losing their jobs, being mocked, being denied public services, and even losing their children. Some witches still live at home and are not comfortable sharing their practice with their parents, grandparents, and/or siblings.

Other witches may fear judgment from their family, friends, partners, or co-workers. Witchcraft is much more easily accepted in most places today than it was just fifty years ago, but there are still misconceptions and closed minds out there. Whether you decide to let people in on your practice or not is your decision and yours alone.

While staying in the broom closet feels safe at times, it can also be constricting. It can be difficult and frustrating to hide your craft, especially in your own home. Coming out of the broom closet can be hard, but it can also lead to meeting other witches and learning from them, working with them, making friends. There are good and bad parts to every choice, but it is your choice to make.

### *Sacred Space*

Sacred space is the space in which you work magick, conduct rituals, meditate, keep an altar, and worship. It can be anywhere, be any size or shape, and it can be temporary or permanent. Some people are lucky enough that they have a whole room dedicated to their sacred space, once you walk through the door you can feel the change. They've devoted the whole room to their witchcraft. Others can only create sacred space for ten minutes in a corner of their bedroom. How your sacred space looks and how big or small it is depends on you and your situation.

If you can only have your sacred space set up for ten minutes or five minutes at a time, that's perfectly fine. If it's at the bathroom sink for that short amount of time, because that's the only way that you can get privacy in your house, that's perfectly fine too. While it would be nice for all of us to have one whole room dedicated to our witchcraft, it's not mandatory, it's not expected, and it's not the norm. Doing what you can with what you've got is a big part of witchcraft, substitutions have to be made now and then and sometimes you have only what's in front of you to use for your craft. This is much more common than you may think.

So how do you create sacred space? Well, once you've picked out where you want to set up your sacred space, be it for your altar, ritual, working magick, or meditation, sacred space is pretty easy to set up. I've found that it's also an intuitive process, finding what helps you get into your magickal mindset and set up your environment to help you achieve your goals. To set up sacred space, be it temporary or permanent, I suggest sweeping and cleaning. The end result doesn't have to do Martha Stewart proud, but just enough so that you don't feel the clutter of dust and things.

Once the space is physically clean, take a large feather, such as a turkey feather, and use that to clean the air of any bad or distracting energies. Similar to sweeping a circle of it's negative or distracting energies, do this to the air with the feather. Then, if you can, light some incense – frankincense, sage, or rosemary – to consecrate the area as sacred space. Sometimes it can help to also sprinkle salt water, light candles, or hang bundles of herbs around, but it's not necessary. This is just a simple, general way to create sacred space. You may find later on that you prefer a different method or add on to this one, it's up to you and whatever you need to do, intuitively, to create that sacred space.

Later on in this book, you'll see that I do this whenever I'm about to raise a circle as well, I find it to be a very helpful exercise to clear my environment as well as my mind before doing rituals. If you feel that you should do this before every meditation, spell, ritual, and divination then do it. It's your craft, only you can know in your gut what's needed to help get you and your environment to that sacred state.

There are some other things to keep in mind when working with your sacred space. Kids and other critters are great, but they can be clumsy and curious. Remember to never leave candles or incense unattended, if you leave the room, put them out. Be mindful of what herbs are hanging around, are they poisonous if ingested? If so, keep them out of reach of kids and pets. Sometimes it helps to have your sacred space as a keep out zone, be it permanent or temporary. When working in your sacred space, you may want to keep pets out for safety, easy clean up, and to keep your concentration. If you are able to have a permanent sacred space, it's a good idea to cleanse and consecrate it every new moon. Cleaning, sweeping, using the feather, and using some incense will do just fine. This way you can get any stagnant energies, dust, and dirt out of there, making it easier for you to work and concentrate.

### *Your Altar*

Your altar is like your work space, much like sacred space, but your altar goes inside your sacred space. An altar is where you make offerings, work magick (although you don't need an altar to do magick), worship, and it is the center point of rituals. Having an altar can benefit you in that it helps you concentrate on what you're doing and it can center you, ground you. You can keep spells (charms, talismans, etc.) on your altar to 'permeate', in that it sits and gains more energy by being there. Once it's been there for a few days, then you can complete the spell or dispose of it, if that's what needs to be done next in the spell.

An altar can hold all of your tools, which is helpful if you're like me and forget where you put things – constantly. If you worship or work with certain deities or spirits, you can have figures or other objects to represent them. Depending on what path you follow, your altar may be more specific. Wiccans tend to have altars that face north, have an item representing their god and goddess, and have an item representing each element. Kitchen witches keep their altars in or near the kitchen if they can (I know there's no room for one in my kitchen if I wanted one there).

Other witches, ones that don't follow a specific path or religion, have a bit more creative freedom with their altars. If your practice doesn't call for specific items and placement of said items on your altar, you can put on your altar whatever speaks to you, whatever you find important, consciously and intuitively. For instance, my altar is set up in layers or rings almost. On the very outside of the altar are two candles, one black, one white, to represent balance and my incense burner (for no reason, that's just where it fits best). Then there is a circle of tools between those candles, these tools are ones that are meaningful to me and ones that I use frequently.

Inside that circle is a semicircle of stones, all of which carry a specific meaning in themselves and for me. There is a rose quartz for love of others, another rose quartz for love of myself, bloodstone for health, tiger's eye for strength and protection, and amethyst for second sight or psychic abilities. In the center of that semicircle is a very small, cast iron cauldron in which I burn herbs and resin incense. This is the set up that works for me. I don't know if it would work for anyone else, but I do know that it works for me, so that's what I use. Play around with your altar, find what works for you.

Finding an altar can be really fun, or a hassle depending on your perspective. Look around your house for things you can use as an altar. End tables, cupboards, shelves, desks, and counter tops all make good altars. You can even use windowsills, bookshelves, and fireplace mantles. Get creative, see what works best for you. Second hand stores are great for finding good altars. I searched high and low for years for a good altar and finally found the perfect one at a second hand store.

For those still in the broom closet, setting up an altar may not be so easy. When you don't want others to know about your practice, it can be difficult to have an altar. You may not be able to have an altar that's set up all the time. Like sacred space, you may have to have your altar up and ready only when you're using it and have the privacy to do so. You may have roommates that don't understand and so you can't even have your tools out, let alone a whole altar. One of the best solutions for this is to, once again, make a trip to a second hand store.

Many second hand stores have old suitcases. If you can find a hard-cased suitcase, that's perfect. Inside the suitcase you can keep all of your books and tools, you can even cover them with a blanket or some sheets to keep them really hidden and protected from damage if someone picks it up.

You can keep the suitcase under your bed or in your closet when you're not using it. When you do need to set up your altar, take all of your tools out of the suitcase, shut the suitcase, and set up your altar on top of it. Just make sure that when you're done, your incense and any charcoal blocks are completely out, don't set your altar on fire. Then put it all back in it's hiding place.

You may find over time that you re-do your altar a lot, that's okay. Sometimes a change is good for energy flow. If you have a permanent altar set up, it's a good idea to cleanse and consecrate it every new moon. A simple sweeping of broom and feather followed by some incense smoke will do the trick.

### *Everyday Witch*

Witchcraft isn't just a hobby, it's a way of life. Once you walk this path you begin to see potential and magick in all sorts of places and things. So how do you work witchcraft into your life as a daily practice? There are several things you can do. As we discussed earlier, meditation, visualization, and daily devotions can help a lot with this, but there are other things that you can do in conjunction with these activities. Here are some things that you can do in your daily life to benefit and enhance your craft.

*Growing Your Own Ingredients.* One thing that can help a lot with your craft, is growing your own plants and herbs. By growing your own magickal ingredients, you're infusing them with the earth's energy while also infusing them with your own energy, linking you to them in a way. It's also helpful to do this, because then you learn more about herbs and plants, what each one looks like, and what they're used for. This is also helpful for conservation. There are some species of sage that are over harvested because they are used so often in occult and new age practices. If you grow your own sage (which is usually easy to grow), then you're not contributing to the over harvesting, but you're still getting the herb that you need.

*Divination.* Practicing divination is both fun and helpful. As explained before, divination is a helpful tool for many people, witches included. By practicing divination regularly, you not only get better at it (understanding what message is being given, what different signs and symbols mean), but it can also help you to see where you're headed on your path. If you don't like what your divinations tell you about where you're headed with your current path, you can always change the outcome. The message given by different forms of divination are often of where you'll be if you continue as you have been going. But this also means that you can change what you're doing and produce a different outcome because of it.

*Spying on the Skies.* Keep track of planetary movements. Record the movements and changes of planets, the moon, and the astrological signs in your book of shadows. Take note of how your mood and energy changes depending on which moon phase or which planet is in your sign. Harvest herbs according to which planet is in which sign. For example: if you want to cast a money spell for a friend, be sure to harvest some mint when Jupiter is in your friend's sign. Furthermore, you can cast that spell for your friend during that time.

*Collecting Tools.* Another thing you can do regularly, is collect your tools. Go on hikes, walk the shoreline, or go for a walk. While you're doing these things you can collect different tools for your craft as well as spell ingredients. Collect some seashells and stones for your altar. Collect wild herbs (be sure you know what you're collecting!) and find bird feathers. Find a small fallen tree branch and make a wand out of it. This way you're connecting with nature (if that's a part of your craft path) and finding natural tools and ingredients for your craft.

*Make Your Own Tools.* Some tools are easier to make than others. You can make a wand out of a fallen branch, which can be easy or difficult, depending on what you want to add to it. If you know how to, you can make your own book of shadows and grimoire (there are a lot of great online sources that can teach you how to do this). If you're really talented with woodwork you can build your own altar. Making your own candles is pretty simple and then you can infuse them with whatever herbs or oils you want (do your research first though!). Depending on what types of skills you already have and what you enjoy doing there are a ton of tools that you can make yourself.

*Daily Devotions and Meditations.* As mentioned before, these are very helpful practices to do on a regular basis. It can be hard sometimes to make the time to do them, but it's very helpful when you do. Daily devotions and meditations can be as simple or complex as you want. You can find them from literary resources, online resources, and books or you can make your own or learn them first hand from someone else.

*Cleansing.* Cleansing is good to do about once a month if you can. It's good to physically clean your environment so that the physical dirt and clutter doesn't clutter up your own energy. When our homes and work areas are clean, we are better able to relax and focus. Once you can get your environment as clean as you feel necessary, do the same to your work area, sacred space, and/or altar. Get any dust and debris out of the way, including old incense ashes (although you can save these for spells and ingredients). However you like to do a cleansing, do that throughout your home and sacred space if you can. It's also wise to cleanse your tools every now and then too, especially if you find them collecting dust for a long time. Cleansing is helpful, but you don't want to do it too often either. It's good for homes, sacred spaces, and tools to collect your energy and to build up their own natural energy. As usual, balance is key.

### Covens

Witchcraft is a fun, exciting, helpful, and fulfilling practice. Some witches find that these aspects of witchcraft can be intensified when you work with others. A coven is a group of witches that work together pretty regularly. Many covens conduct rituals, seances, magick, divinations, and even study groups together. It can be really fulfilling to talk to other witches and work with them too. It's nice to not feel so alone on your path sometimes. Covens can also help you to stay dedicated to your path if you feel that you're falling into a rut. Not only that, but covens can help do spells with you, adding more energy and more power to your spells.

Covens can be wonderful, but it's a good idea to be careful when finding a coven. There are some groups out there that call themselves covens, but their motives are hidden. Some people, disguised as covens, are looking to victimize and manipulate people. When joining a coven be sure you know who is a part of it and be sure that you can really trust them. You don't have to join the first coven you find. Talk to the members, get to know them, become friends with them first. Not everyone is a monster, but it's always good to be careful. If a coven frowns upon or outright forbids asking questions or having a say in what goes on with the coven, then you may want to heavily reconsider being a part of that coven. You should always have a say in your own path, in your own life.

Finding a coven can be very tricky at times. Depending on where you live and what kind of community you live in, it can be either very easy to find a coven or rather difficult. There are some websites out there that can help, such as witchvox.com, so you can always try those and see what turns up. I lived in a couple of small towns in Pennsylvania over the space of fifteen years (fifteen long, long years) and you would think that these small towns that have more Catholic and Christian churches than businesses would be pretty devoid of covens or any witch activity.

Not likely. I found a good handful of witches while living in Pennsylvania. Don't get me wrong, these small towns weren't bursting at the seams with witches, but there were some witches and some covens that were quite helpful. Then, I moved to Eugene, Oregon which, I've found, is much more open minded and accepting than the small Pennsylvania towns I was used to. I thought there would be witches and covens all over the place. Not likely – at least so far. I've looked a few places and checked out witchvox.com, but it would seem there's more witchcraft activity up in Portland, a nice two hour drive away.

When joining a coven, be sure to stay honest to yourself. If you find that your coven participates in certain practices (skyclad for example) and you're not comfortable with it, be honest with yourself and your coven. If you're not comfortable in your coven, your magick won't be as effective, but more than that, you should be comfortable in your practice. Don't sacrifice yourself for others, it will leave you unhappy and unfulfilled which isn't good for you or your craft. If you're afraid to be honest with your coven about these things, maybe it's time to reconsider being a part of that coven, because a coven is like a family, you should be able to be open, honest, and comfortable with them. And there's nothing wrong with reconsidering being a part of a coven, it doesn't mean you're weaker than them or one of you is wrong, it just means that you see things differently, and that's okay.

So, if you're looking for a coven or just a simple study group, keep your eyes open and your ears perked, because many times you'll find witches in the most unlikely places.

### *A Solitary Witch*

Coven life isn't for everyone. Some of us like to take the more hermetic path or, depending on where we live, we don't have much of a choice but to practice alone. Solitary witchcraft is just as good as group witchcraft, no worries. Whether you choose the solitary life or the solitary life chooses you, you can still work powerful and effective witchcraft. It can be difficult working as a solitary witch sometimes. You may experience things or read things that you find very exciting, but there's no one to share it with. You may want some help with a spell, an extra boost of energy from someone else, but there's no one to help you. It can be hard, disheartening, and sometimes lead to a rut, but there's a bright side too.

When working as a solitary witch, you have more freedom to practice the craft the way that you want to practice it. It's easier to conduct ritual when you're a solitary witch, because the only person's schedule you have to take into account is your own. If you're much more comfortable working alone, an introvert or if you're shy or still in the broom closet, solitary witchcraft may be more your style. There are many witches who benefit more from being a solitary witch rather than working with others. This can be attributed to only having to focus on you and your own experiences, honing in on your abilities, strengths, and progress.

Some may find this selfish, but it is your path and how you decide to walk it is your own. There's no shame or harm in working alone. It's not selfish or weird. I find that working alone has often helped bring me clarity and peace of mind, but that's just me. Even if you are a solitary witch, that doesn't mean you have to work alone all the time. You can always get together with other witches for spells or celebrating the seasons, it's all up to you. Only you can know which way works best for you.

# 5 DIVINATION

We've already talked about divination quite a bit so far. We know what it is and what it's used for, but we haven't gone quite in depth with it yet. There are many different forms of divination, some easier than others, some more difficult, some general, and some more intricate. In this chapter we'll focus on several different forms of divination. I'll explain each one in some depth and if you find that you are interested in one of them do some more research on it. There are a lot of great resources on divination out there.

### *Tarot*

Each tarot card deck is made up of 78 cards. The first 22 cards are called the Major Arcana. The Major Arcana cards depict the Fool's journey, a life journey that we all experience. Along his journey, the Fool meets important archetypes and comes to find lessons in those meetings as well as his journey onward. The 56 remaining cards are called the Minor Arcana. The Minor Arcana is constructed of four suits: Wands, Cups, Swords, and Pentacles. Similar to a playing card deck, there is ace through 10 and then Knight, Queen, Prince, Princess (some decks have Knight, Queen, King, Page).

Each suit represents an element and therefore also represent the astrological signs. The Wands represent fire, the Cups represent water, Swords to air, and Pentacles to earth. Every deck has different imagery and therefore one deck can have slightly different meanings or vastly different meanings compared to another deck. Use whatever meanings that come with the deck that you buy or receive. Before jumping in and starting a spread, I suggest that you go through and look at each card as well as read each card's meaning. You don't have to memorize it, just familiarize yourself with it.

Some tarot readers work very hard to memorize their tarot deck's meanings, that way they don't have to always reference a book when doing readings. Some feel that it ruins the feel or ambiance of a reading when you use a book during a reading. Other tarot readers continuously use a book during their readings, even after reading for many years. After twelve years of reading tarot cards, I still use a book. As I mentioned before, I have a degree in criminal justice. When I was in my third year of college I interned with a police department as a public safety aide, working side by side with police on patrol. Officers who had been on the force for twenty plus years still read people their Miranda Rights from a card that they carried with them.

These police officers did this because they didn't want to risk missing something if they gave the Miranda Rights from memory. If they missed something, even just one line, it could be used in court to the defendant's benefit. I view reading tarot cards in a very similar way. Each card has a specific meaning, so if I tried to read the cards and their meanings from memory, I might miss something. By missing something I might completely misread the spread, missing some important message. Not wanting to take that chance, I like to use the book that came with my cards. Again, this is just personal preference.

Many tarot readers, including myself, will tell you that each tarot deck has an energy of it's own. It's good to shuffle your deck regularly, even if you're not going to read them, just to get your energy mixed in there. There is a big question about what source of energy or intelligence is coming through the cards. Is it spirits, god, your subconscious? There is no right or wrong answer to this, because no one really knows. Personally, I think it's the creative/destructive force that runs through our universe, that created our universe. The cards, like many divination tools, serve as a medium between you and that energy. The cards allow you to tap into it to see what's going on.

Tarot cards can tell your fortune or misfortune, but more often the cards simply lay out for you what's going on in your current situation. The outcome shown is the outcome that will befall you if you continue the way you've been going, but that means that there is room for change. If you change how you act and react to your situation, you can change your outcome, if you want to. Tarot cards are a wonderful tool. I love my cards very much. They've gotten me out of a couple of messy situations and have many times helped me to find clarity. I recommend the tarot to anyone who's interested.

I have a list of tarot tips on my blog if you're interested. My blog is listed at the end of this book in part 3. There are many more tarot resources out there in books, online, and even at some workshops.

### *Runes*

Runes are the ancient alphabet that was used in many Germanic countries many, many years ago. There are a total of 24 runes and 1 blank rune, totaling 25 in a set. Like the tarot, the runes can answer your specific questions or they can give you a general reading of where you are right now in your current situation. Each rune has it's own meaning, specific to it. Depending on where the runes fall and how closely together determines the answers to your questions.

Like the tarot, rune readers often use spreads. These spreads are drawn out on paper or cloth and laid out, then the reader will cast the runes onto the spreads. The runes will fall along the drawn spread to show which rune means what depending on where it is and how close it is to other runes. Runes can be a bit trickier to read than tarot cards sometimes, because you cast them instead of place them down. You never quite know where they're going to land and it's up to the reader to interpret the runes' meanings based on where they've fallen.

Runes come on all sorts of materials. There are runes made from clay, beautiful stones, perfectly round bits of wood, acorns, glass, and even sea shells. You can even make your own runes if you want to. Because runes are small and can be easily lost, it's a good idea to keep them in a drawstring bag, tied up tight. We've moved three times in the past year, and because of it we're still finding my boyfriend's runes in random boxes and pockets.

### *Pendulums*

Pendulums are said to be similar to Ouija and spirit boards because you can contact spirits and ancestors with them. A pendulum is a stone, crystal, or even a key tied to the end of a chain or string. Holding the chain or string between your thumb and pointer finger, you ask the pendulum which way means yes. The pendulum will start to move either left to right or forward and back. Once it's done this, ask which way means no. It will then start to move in the perpendicular direction of the yes motion.

From this point you can ask yes/no questions and get your answers. There are some pendulum boards out there that you can use also. These pendulum boards have more answers on them, giving you a more elaborate way of communication. Some people believe that pendulums don't really work, that you yourself are causing the pendulum to move through an ideomotor effect. This means that you are subconsciously moving the pendulum into the direction that you know is the answer or is the answer that you want to hear.

This may be true, but I used a pendulum to determine the date of birth of my second nephew. I simply asked, "Will he be born on the..." and then I plugged in a number of the month the doctors said he would be born. The pendulum only moved in the direction of yes when I got to the 22nd and then did not do it again as I continued forward into the month. As it turns out, my nephew was born on the 22nd. Now my subconscious is either a really good guesser or there was some sort of connection there between my subconscious and the spirits or the energy that runs through our universe.

Because this divination method often works with spirits, it's always good to be respectful. Don't taunt the spirits or call them liars. If you're not getting correct answers to the questions you know the answers to and it seems like it's a faulty connection, simply state your thanks and end the session. If you work closely with spirits in your practice, you may also want to leave an offering as a thank you to the spirits/gods.

### *Crystal Ball*

Crystal balls can be very tricky to work with. Some believe that you can only use true crystal to use as a crystal ball. Others say that you can use glass, amethyst, or some other clear-ish stone. The trick to using a crystal ball for divination is to stare into it, focusing your attention onto the crystal ball until images come to you through it. I have never tried to use a crystal ball, but from what I've read it can be a very difficult style of divination to master.

It's good to keep your crystal ball wrapped in silk or velvet and kept out of the sun. It's said that letting it sit in the moonlight is good for it, that it helps strengthen it's energies. The main way to tell the difference between glass and crystal balls are the bubbles inside. If there are bubbles inside the globe, then it's glass. However, true crystal balls can be very, very expensive.

### *Witch's Glass*

Using a witch's glass is very similar to using a crystal ball. Once centered and focused, you gaze into the glass, awaiting images to come forth. Some believe that you have to be in a trance state and using these tools to receive messages. Others believe that as long as you concentrate and are patient enough, the messages will come through. Witch's glass is a concave bit of glass that is painted black on the side that the glass comes out (think the outside of a bowl).

Propped up at an angle, you place the glass on a bit of black cloth and then gaze into the glass. Similar to a crystal ball, you don't expose a witch's glass to the sun, but it helps to expose it to the moonlight. Keep it wrapped in cloth when you're not using it and out of the sunlight. It's quite easy to make a witch's glass if you can't find or can't afford one. Once again, head on over to your local second hand store and find an old clock. Most older clocks have concave glass that rests over the face of a clock.

Remove the glass and paint the outside of it black. You may have to use a couple of coats to get it to a solid black. What's great about making your own is that you can infuse herbs into the paint to help with your divination. Once the paint is dry, let the witch's glass lay under the light of a full moon, then store it as instructed above.

### *Tea Leaves and Coffee Grounds*

As mentioned before, many cultures use tea leaves and coffee grounds as a form of divination. The patterns left in the leaves and grounds can give us clues on what's going on in our lives and what's to come. This form of divination can also be a tricky one at times as it may be difficult to pick out what shapes and symbols are in the leaves and grounds. But as with most things, the more you do it, the easier it gets. The more often you read tea leaves and/or coffee grounds, the easier it will be to pick out the messages in them.

There are different ways of reading the leaves and grounds, but the most basic way that I've learned is what I have here. I don't have a lot of experience in reading tea leaves or coffee grounds, but I do know that it is a very old form of divination and that it can be very helpful. Drink your coffee or tea until there is only one sip of left of the drink. Then, turn your cup over onto it's saucer and turn it three times. Flip the cup back over and look for symbols in the leaves or grounds.

As I said, there are other ways of reading the leaves and grounds. There are even tea cups out there that have different symbols and placements painted on them to help you read the leaves and grounds better.

### *Playing Cards*

Many people read playing cards similarly to the way tarot cards are read. Each card has it's own meaning and each suit has it's own characteristics. Playing cards are also read in spreads, just like the tarot. Tarot spreads can be used for playing cards, but there are also spreads made just for playing cards. Sometimes a card's meaning can be changed or slightly altered depending on what other cards it is near in the spread.

This is another old form of divination. My great grandmother and her mother used to read playing cards, but I was never taught how to (long family story). There are books out there though that can teach you how to read playing cards. If you have a deck of cards you want to use as a divination tool, find a book with the meanings in them and then write the meanings on the cards themselves, or you can just keep a small notebook with the meanings in them.

### *Ouija and Spirit Boards*

We've all heard about Ouija boards and spirit boards. Many of us have heard different myths and warnings about them as well. These boards are known as being direct ways of communicating with spirits. Because of this, there's a lot of fear floating around them. As with any tool of divination or spirit communication, always be respectful and don't provoke any spirits/gods. Some people believe that these boards can become doorways for demons and poltergeists to come through into our world. As long as you are careful and respectful you shouldn't have a problem.

I've used Ouija boards throughout my life and have never had a negative experience. An old friend of mine in high school claimed that she felt ill and extremely anxious, like something was after her, but that could have also just been because she was excited and scared. But who knows, maybe it was something. Either way, we took the Ouija board out to the woods and burned it. Apparently, this is something you should never do, because if you hear the board scream or cry as it's burning it's supposed to be an omen of your death soon to come. Luckily, we didn't hear anything.

Some advice I have for those using Ouija boards is to always be respectful, never provoke the spirits, never ask the spirits to move something or prove they're there, never use one alone, and always say goodbye. It's said that when you ask the spirits to move something or prove that they're there, you're inviting them in, giving them power. Something you don't want to do if you don't really know who or what you're talking to. Saying goodbye is always important because it 'seals' the board and ends the session. When you say goodbye, move the planchette over the words 'goodbye' and say goodbye aloud.

It is said that if you use a Ouija board alone, you're able to be possessed, whereas when you use it with someone else you are less likely to be influenced or possessed because someone else's energy is anchoring you. This is another tool that is said to be influenced by the ideomotor effect, so when using one be sure to keep that in mind. It's also a good idea to use a Ouija or spirit board with someone you know well and trust. You don't want to have a session with someone who is likely to move the planchette in order to get a rise out of you or to 'enhance' the moment.

# 6 Magick

There has been a lot of mention about magick thus far, theories on how it works and what it is, but now it's time to go more in depth with it. There are many different forms of magick, all of which are helpful in their own ways. This chapter will address different forms of magick and how to create each type. Later on, in part 2 of this book, I will give you a peek into my own grimoire with different spells, charms, and more.

### *Charms, Amulets, and Talismans*

There are many different definitions for each of these things. Often, they are used synonymously. For the purposes of this book, I will list below how I define each one. Later on, if you find that you like a different definition better, then go with that.

*Charms:* These are bags or pouches of magickal ingredients used for positive outcomes, protection, and banishing.

*Amulets:* These are items, such as jewelry, that are infused with a spell to draw a specific type of energy to you. (A love amulet would draw loving energies to you; a prosperity amulet would draw money).

*Talismans:* This is a symbol or object that represents your power or the power of your spirits/god/goddess. This can be a bit of jewelry, an object you carry in your pocket, or even a tattoo.

To make a charm you lay out all of your magickal ingredients along with an appropriately colored pouch or small drawstring bag. Charge (infuse) each item with your intent by holding it in your hands and visualizing your goal. You can chant or speak your intention and then continue to visualize your intended outcome as you place each item into the pouch or bag. You can carry the charm with you or keep it in a specific place.

To make an amulet, you would find the item you want to make an amulet first. Once you've chosen the item, place it in a small dish. Once again, charge your magickal ingredients by holding them and visualizing your intent. Then cover the item with the herbs, oils, and whatever other ingredients you've charged. You can chant or state your intention as you do this. Depending on what the amulet is for, you can leave it in the moon or sunlight for however many days you wish or keep it on your altar for a few days to soak up the energy that it needs. Carry or wear the amulet to attract the energies of your spell's intention.

To make a talisman, similarly to an amulet, you find an object that represents your power or the power of the spirits/gods/goddesses that you work with. If this talisman is for your own power, infuse it with your energy. Concentrate on the object as you either hold it in your hands or lay it on your altar with your hands over it. Imagine your power coming out of your hands in a bright light which is absorbed by the object. If you work with spirits or deities, ask that they bless the item in their name, do any offerings or chants that you need to do as well. Wear the talisman to help focus your own power, amplify your power, draw on the energy of your spirits or deities, or to honor them.

### *Poppets*

Poppets are like little dolls, but you make these dolls yourself from cloth. They don't have to be perfect and they don't have to be pretty. Poppets can be used for all sorts of magick. They can be used for banishing, attraction, binding, and more. Fill the doll with your magickal ingredients that have been charged with your intent. Whoever the poppet is for, be sure to include a bit of their hair, blood, saliva, or fingernails into the poppet. For example: If you wanted to banish someone from your life you would use a bit of their hair. But if you wanted to banish a bad habit of yours, you would include a bit of the habit (such as some tobacco) as well as a bit of your hair or fingernails. Depending on what the poppet is for, you dispose of it or keep it in a different way. Poppets for banishing are burned, while poppets for attraction are left out in the open.

### *Spell Bottles and Spell Jars*

Spell bottles and jars are great forms of magick. They're easy and fun to do. You are essentially creating a bottled spell, one that you hold onto and keep for as long as you need it. Having a couple of spell bottles collected on a shelf or table also does for some nice decoration as you can use any jar or bottle you want, and there are some cool ones out there. For a spell bottle or jar, you collect the appropriate ingredients for your spell and charge them with your intent. Then you fill the bottle or jar with those ingredients while visualizing your goal, chanting, and/or stating your intent.

Like poppets, spell bottles are handled differently depending on the spell. Home protection spell bottles are usually buried outside your front door (in the ground or in a flower pot). Home happiness spell bottles are kept in the heart of the home and power spell bottles are kept at your altar or in your sacred space.

### *Witch's Ladder and Witch's Ball*

These two magickal tools are for the same purpose, protection. A witch's ladder is made from yarn and feathers, then hung in the highest point in your home to protect it. A witch's ball is a glass ball, usually decorated with multiple colors, and hung in a window, usually a front window. The witch's ball is said to act somewhat like a dream catcher, but instead of catching nightmares, it catches negative energy, curses, and evil spirits. If you know how to blow glass, you could make your own witch's ball, but if not, most occult and witchcraft stores carry them.

Witch's ladders are fairly easy to make. You need three lengths of yarn, one black, one white, and one red. Braid these yarns together into a large ring. Then, sew nine feathers (they don't all have to be the same feathers, they look rather nice with different feathers) into the braided ring. As you put all of this together, imagine your home protected from intrusion, harm, and destruction. Once you're done sewing in the nine feathers, hang the ladder at the highest point in your home.

### *Candle Spells*

Candle spells are really great for complicated goals and other goals that need a lot of energy put into them. Candle spells tend to last a very long time, because they're not done until the candle has burned itself out. Candles good for candle spells are usually small tapers (very common in occult stores) or votive candles. Don't use a pillar candle unless it's a goal that you know is going to take a long time, this way you can be constantly putting energy and intent into that goal.

To create a spell candle, pick a candle that is the appropriate color for your spell. You can dress the candle in the appropriate oil if you like, along with the appropriate herbs. Be sure to also carve any symbols or even just one word that embodies your goal. Keep the candle at your altar and meditate over it whenever you can, visualizing your desired outcome. Do not leave the candle burning unattended. When you're done meditating on it for now, snuff out or blow out the wick.

*Note: some witches believe that when doing candle spells you should never blow out the wick, that you should always snuff it out, otherwise the energy diffuses. Then there are those who believe that by blowing out the candle, some of that energy is released towards that goal, a little bit each time you meditate, give it energy, and then blow it out, sending the energy out with the smoke toward your goal. It is up to you which you find works better. You can always experiment to see which one works for you.*

If you have a chant or a spoken intention, do so as you meditate over the spell candle. When it's the last meditation for the spell candle, when it's at it's lowest point and about to die, let it burn itself out. Continue your visualizations, chants, and/or spoken intentions until the candle burns itself out. Then bury the remaining wax. These spells are more long term, so be sure to stay patient.

### *Oils*

Oils are great for quick, simple results. Oils, because they're derived from plants and herbs, have the same associations as plants and herbs. You can mix essential oils for a goal along with a carrier oil (grape seed oil for example) and wear the oil to attract certain energies. You can also dress candles and certain ritual tools with oils (be sure to wash them clean when you're done) and you can use oils for anointing yourself and others for rituals.

When using essential oils, a carrier oil is needed. The carrier oil acts as a base, spreading the essential oils farther, like a filler. This is also very helpful because some essential oils are not good for you in pure form. Some oils in pure form can damage your skin or cause an allergic type reaction. Be sure to do your research before using essential oils, know what you're using, the effects they can have on your skin and body, and whether or not you're allergic to them.

### *Herbal Blends*

Herbal blends can be very helpful for spells, rituals, and meditations. These are simply a blend of herbs that you use for a specific intent. So a love blend would contain multiple herbs used for love spells. A peace blend would contain multiple herbs for peace. You can create these herbal blends and then hold onto them, keep them until you use them. For example: you can create a ritual blend for your rituals specifically and then use that blend whenever you do ritual.

Herbal blends can be scattered across an altar or a sacred space, used in a spell, or burned on a self-igniting charcoal block. Be sure that the herbs you use are not toxic and are safe to burn. If the herbs are toxic, don't ingest them and make sure kids and pets can't get a hold of it. If the herbs aren't safe to burn, don't burn them, just keep them on your altar or in your charm pouch or spell bottle.

### *Chants*

Chanting can be very helpful for all sorts of magick and meditation. Chants are words of intention that rhyme. Rhyming can help to focus your mind and even help you to enter a trance state. Repeating chants over and over can help you to send your energy towards your intended goal. Some spells come with chants, but you can always create your own as well. While chants can be helpful for some, others may prefer spoken intention, which is basically stating your intention clearly.

Others find speaking at all during spellwork or meditation to be distracting. Sometimes just focusing on your intent and your actions is all you need. Find what works for you, everyone works differently.

### *Some Helpful Hints and Tips*

*Don't leave candles burning by themselves

*Expectations will only slow you down. Don't expect great, wonderful things to happen during whatever you're doing, but don't expect nothing to happen either. Go into it blind, every time, this way you're not only expecting one certain thing and therefore missing what else is going on or becoming frustrated when nothing happens.

*Charging stones – not in the sun! Some stones fade in the sun, it's best to charge them under the moon instead of the sun.

*Feathers and Cats – Enough said.

*Meeting other practitioners – Stay Safe!

*Be careful with oils, use carrier oils

*Be careful with certain herbs, plants, and foods

~Cinnamon can irritate the skin.

~Lemon juice on the skin can make you more prone to sunburn.

~Know what you're allergic to and what others are allergic to if you're helping someone else.

~Do your homework: before using stones, herbs, plants, and oils find out first if it's poisonous/toxic.

*Be respectful when working with spirits, gods, and ancestors

*Be thankful

*Second hand shopping is your friend

*Don't be too hard on yourself, some days will be easier than others. You don't have to be perfect or the best. As long as you do the best you can, you're golden (and that goes for every aspect of life).

*While spells are very helpful, they should never be used as a substitute for therapy, medical assistance, or safety. If you need help medically and/or emotionally, seek the help of a doctor and/or a therapist or counselor. If someone is harassing or hurting you, go to the police, a shelter, or an adult that you can trust. No one has the right to make you feel threatened or fearful. There is no shame in asking for help – ever.

*At some point you'll probably hit a rut, most people do. That's okay, you'll find your way out of it eventually. Sometimes, when in a rut, it helps to go back to the beginning. What first drew you to witchcraft?

*Never stop learning. Keep reading books, talking to other practitioners, learning about other religions/spiritualities/paths. Try new things. Go to workshops if you can.

*Don't let the internet be your only source of information, there's a lot of misinformation on the internet.

*Be critical when reading. Don't tear everything you read apart, but be skeptical. It's healthy to think critically, but remember to also keep an open mind.

# Plants & Herb Appendix

### *A*

Acorn: Growth, strength, hunting

Alfalfa: Money, prosperity

Allspice: Luck, lust, healing, compassion

Almond: Anger management, prosperity, money, wisdom

Aloe Vera: Protection

Anise: Prophetic dreams

Apple: Heartbreak management, love, divination, hunting

Avocado: Beauty, money

### *B*

Basil: Business success, courage, prosperity, protection, money, fortune telling, inner strength

Bay: Success, knowing the future, wisdom

Bayberry: Employment

Bay Laurel: To induce dreams, protection, psychic ability

Bay Leaf: Employment, mental powers, prosperity, protection, strength, victory, wishes

Bergamot: Employment, sexual harassment management, luck, curse breaking

Bittersweet: Heartbreak management

Blackberry: Protection, healing

Bluebell: Education

Blueberry: Protection, the occult

Buckeye: Gambling

Buckthorn: Legal matters, finances

## C

Cactus: Protection

Camphor: Sexual assault harassment, occult knowledge, psychic ability, past lives

Caraway: Education, theft, calmness, stress management, meditation

Cardamom: Love, friendship, persuasion, lust

Carnation: Strength

Catnip: Anger management, beauty, depression management, love, fun, animal magick

Cattail: Lust

Cedar: Prosperity

Celandine: Legal matters

Celery: Mental and psychic power, weight loss

Chamomile: Anger management, to induce dreams, to prevent nightmares, prophetic dreams, sleep, stress management, health, meditation, calmness, luck

Cherry: Love

Chicory: Liberation

Chili: Lust, excitement, virility, new ideas, protection from evil spirits

Chives: Relaxation, positive perception, breaking bad habits

Cinnamon: Love, lust, psychic ability, success, power, knowledge

Citronella: Removing obstacles, happiness, thinking clearly

Clover: Luck, prosperity, success, happy relationships

Cloves: Education, gossip management, love, lust, mental powers, prophetic dreams, protection, removing curses and curse breaking

Corn: Virility, lust, friendship, harvest

Cucumber: Prosperity, chastity

Cumin: Physical protection, preventing bad luck, spiritual protection

Cypress: Hunting, liberation

## D

Daisy: Depression management, love

Daffodil: Love

Dandelion: Divination, psychic ability, wishes

Dill: Lust, protection, overcoming obstacles, helping children, positive perspective

Dogwood: Wishes

Dragon's Blood: Courage, protection

## E

Elder: Theft

Eucalyptus: Healing, lucid dreaming, protection

Eyebright: Mental powers, memory, divination, truth telling

## F

Fennel: Motherhood, inner strength, courage, education, healing

Fern: Beauty, education, luck

Feverfew: Travel, physical protection, health, inner strength

Flax: Healing, psychic ability

Frankincense: Sacredness, cleansing, consecration

## G

Gardenia: Love

Garlic: Health, theft, banishing, curse-breaking, inner strength, protection

Geranium: Love

Ginger: Apathy, love, success, money, business success

Ginseng: Beauty, health, lust

Goldenrod: Divination

Goldenseal: Healing, inner strength

## H

Hawthorn: Business success, depression management, health, wishes, fertility, lust, protection, fairy magick

Hazel: Luck, wisdom, wishes

Hazelnut: Divination, luck, protection

Heather: Luck

Hemlock: Protection against negative energies and spirits, astral projection

Hibiscus: Divination

Hickory: Legal matters

High John: Success, victory

Holly: Luck

Hops: To induce dreams, stress management

Honey: Sex, love, friendship, peace

Honeysuckle: Depression management, heartbreak management, psychic ability

## I

Irish Moss: Luck, business success, gambling

Ivy: Protection, divination, health

## J

Jasmine: Romance, love, meditation, to induce dreams, fortune telling, heartbreak management, prophetic dreams

Juniper: Hunting, moon magick, protection, theft, psychic awareness

## L

Lavender: Peace, calm, anger management, creativity, to induce dreams, liberation, love, menopause, protection, friendship, happiness

Lemon: Friendship, anti-negativity, exams, longevity

Lemon Balm: Depression management, health, heartbreak management, love, mental powers, success

Lemongrass: Lust, psychic powers

Licorice: Education, communicating with ancestors, helping ghosts move on, love

Lilac: Protection

Lily of the Valley: Depression management

Loosestrife: Peace

Lotus: Health, liberation, love

## *M*

Magnolia: Heartbreak management

Mandrake *Toxic*: Prosperity, fertility, strength, protection, power amplifier

Marigold: Legal matters, psychic ability

Marjoram: Depression management, grieving, moving on, inner strength, happiness

Meadowsweet: Divination, love

Mint: Anger management, healing, love, prophetic dreams

Mistletoe: Liberation, love, romance, protection from evil, conception, dreaming, hunting

Morning Glory: Depression management, peace

Mugwort: Courage, divination, to induce dreams, healing, prophetic dreams, protection, psychic ability, strength

Mulberry: Strength, wisdom

Mullein: Courage, nightmare prevention

Mustard: Protecting, purification

Myrrh: Healing, consecration

Myrtle: Love

## *N*

Nettle: Gossip management, protection, stress management, healing, curse breaking

Nutmeg: Health, love, luck, mental powers, psychic ability, fortune telling, money

## O

Oak: Healing, hunting, luck

Oats: Stress management

Olive: Healing, victory

Onion: Healing, beauty

Orange: Friendship, success

Oregano: Astral projection, health, happiness

## P

Pansy: Love

Parsley: Speaking to the dead, lust, mental powers, fertility, cleansing, telling the truth

Passionflower: Anger management, stress management

Patchouli: Enemies, virility, sexual energy, fertility, divination, money

Peach: Heartbreak management, youth

Pecan: Employment

Pennyroyal: Strength, physical protection, money

Pepper (Black): Protection, inner strength, banishing

Pepper (Red): Love, sex, telling the truth, self-confidence, health

Peppermint: Health, menopause, psychic ability, sleep, healing relationships, calming bad situations, anti-jealousy

Pine: Employment, gambling, health, hunting, protection, induce dreams

Pomegranate: Divination, education, luck

Poppy: Love, divination, sleep, fertility

## R

Rose: Love, romance, anger management, beauty, luck

Rosemary: Beauty, cleansing, consecrating, protection, nightmare prevention, health, love, lust, mental powers, theft, banish negativity, memory

Rowan: Health, success, wisdom

Rue: Education, gossip management, health

## S

Saffron: Health

Sage: Protection, cleansing, purification, hunting, menopause, mental powers, wisdom, animal magick

Salt: Purification, protection

Sandalwood: Business success, health, mental powers

Skullcap: Anxiety management, induce dreams, sleep

Slippery Elm: Enemies, gossip management

Snake Root: Luck

Snap Dragon: Gossip management, prosperity

Spearmint: Mental powers

Star Anise: Consecration, purification, curse breaking, luck, happiness

St. John's Wort: Courage, strength, stress management

Strawberry: Heartbreak management

Sunflower: Friendship, prosperity, wisdom, wishes

Sweet Pea: Courage, friendship

## T

Tarragon: Self-confidence, dragon magick

Thistle: Courage, health, strength, fairies

Thyme: Courage, health, love, psychic ability, sleep

Tonka Bean: Friendship

## V

Valerian: Anxiety management, creativity, love, sleep, peace, friendship, dreams

Vanilla: Friendship, hunting, love, lust, wishes

Vervain: Anger management, love, sexual harassment management, sleep, wishes, peace, healing, psychic protection, magick to help children

Violet: Health, love, luck, lust, wishes

## W

Walnut: Desirability, mental powers, fertility, wishes

Wheat: Fertility, money, prosperity

Willow: Health, love, protection

Wintergreen: Health

Witch Hazel: Beauty, protection, sexual harassment management

Wolfbane: Protection

Wood Betony: Nightmare prevention

Wormwood: Healing, protection from evil spirits, psychic ability

## Y

Yarrow: Courage, heartbreak management, love

# STONE APPENDIX

## A

Abalone: Prosperity

Agate: Courage

Agate (Banded): Health, physical energy, physical strength

Agate (Blue): Depression management, peace

Agate (Green): Business success, gardening, health, prosperity

Agate (Leopard Skin): Stress management

Agate (Moss): Gardening, growth

Alexandrite: Psychic attack management

Amazonite: Creativity, gambling, success

Amber: Beauty, love, luck, money, peace, physical strength, protection

Amethyst: Anger management, courage, divination, to induce dreams, health, justice, love, peace, psychic ability, stress management, wisdom

Ametrine: Change, meditation

Apache Tear: Protection

Aquamarine: Cleansing, courage, peace, psychic ability, travel

Aventurine: Business success, creativity, education, gambling, health, mental ability

Azurite: Divination, to induce dreams, psychic ability

## B

Bloodstone: Health, business success, courage, magickal power, money, physical strength, prosperity

## C

Calcite (Orange): Amplification, creativity, joy, magickal power

Carnelian: Anger management, courage, education, eloquence, health, lust, mental ability, money, peace, protection

Cat's Eye: Beauty

Chrysoprase: Friendship, joy, stress management, success

Citrine: Creativity, to induce dreams, nightmare prevention, mental ability, protection, psychic ability

Coral: Health, lust, peace, protection, wisdom

## D

Diamond: Health, protection, courage, physical strength

## E

Emerald: Business success, to induce dreams, love, mental ability, prosperity, protection, psychic ability

## F

Flint: Health, protection

Flourite: Mental ability, psychic ability, psychic attack management

## G

Garnet: Health, physical energy, physical strength, protection, theft

Geode: Childbirth, meditation

## H

Hematite: Courage, divination, grounding, health, justice, meditation, psychic attack management

Holey Stone/Hag Stone: Health, protection, luck

## J

Jade: Business success, courage, gardening, health, love, prosperity, protection, wisdom, stress management

Jasper: Beauty, health, protection

Jet: Luck, psychic ability

## K

Kunzite: Depression management, grounding

## L

Lapis Lazuli: Business success, psychic ability, spirituality, wisdom

Lepidolite: Anger management, nightmare prevention, peace, spirituality

## M

Malachite: Business success, gardening

Marble: Protection, success

Moonstone: Childbirth, dieting, divination, grounding, bad habit management, love, protection

Mother of Pearl: Childbirth, prosperity, protection

## O

Obsidian (Black): Grounding, bad habit management, peace, protection, psychic ability

Obsidian (Rainbow): Divination

Obsidian (Snowflake): To induce dreams

Onyx: Bad habit management, peaceful separation

Opal: Beauty, change, creativity, divination, to induce dreams, luck, prosperity, psychic attack management

## P

Pearl: Love, luck, prosperity, protection

Peridot: Health, prosperity, protection, to induce dreams

## Q

Quartz (Clear): Amplification, divination, gardening, health, magickal power, meditation, mental ability, peace, physical energy, protection psychic ability, purification, spirituality, wisdom

Quartz (Rose): Beauty, friendship, love, peace

Quartz (Smoky): Health

## R

Ruby: Nightmare prevention, magickal power, prosperity, protection

## S

Sapphire: Health, love, peace, prosperity

Sunstone: Health, joy, physical energy, protection

## T

Tiger's Eye: Gambling, justice, luck, physical energy, protection

Topaz (Blue): Dieting

Topaz (Smoky): Protection

Topaz (Yellow): Anger management, creativity, health

Tourmaline (Black): Grounding, peaceful separation, protection

Tourmaline (Blue): Peace

Tourmaline (Green): Business success, justice, money, prosperity

Tourmaline (Pink): Friendship, justice

Tourmaline (Watermelon): Change

Turquoise: Friendship, health, luck, protection, psychic ability

## U

Unakite: Beauty, change, joy

## Color Appendix

Red: Courage, personal strength, willpower, creativity, art, justice, love, sex, attraction, purification, activity, vitality, fire

Orange: Attraction, education, business, proposals, creativity, love, sex, health, purification

Yellow: Communication, creativity success, joy, air, art, education, mental abilities

Gold: Creativity, art, money, prosperity, financial security, purification

Green: Growth, fertility, prosperity, earth, dreams, emotional health, love, sex, attraction, luck, money, financial security, physical health

Blue-Green: Dreams

Teal: Handling practical matters, making decisions, achieving balance

Aqua: Emotional health

Turquoise: Stress relief, education, memory, logic, problem solving

Light Blue: Clearing the mind, calmness, peace, tranquility, healing, pleasant dreams, physical healing

Blue: Wisdom, dreams, protection, psychic ability

Dark Blue: Organization, structure, water, emotional health, justice

Purple: Spirituality, mental ability, psychic power

Violet: Creativity, art, peace

Royal Purple: Justice

Lavender: Intellect, soothe erratic energy, inner beauty radiates outward

Pink: Romantic love, friendship, harmony

Peach: Kindness, gentleness, sympathy, empathy, well-wishing

Mauve: Intuition, self-trust, self-confidence

Brown: Grounding, centering, common sense, stability, diffusing harmful situations, education, justice

Black: Separation, wisdom, hiding things, emotional healing, justice, psychic abilities, banishing

Silver: Creativity, art, money, prosperity, financial security, protection, psychic abilities

Gray: Dreams, emotional health

White: Clarity, spirituality, spiritual guidance, education, protection, psychic abilities

# Part Two – A Peek at my Grimoire

**Meditation Exercises**

*Exercise 1*

Sit comfortably in a chair or on the floor with something solid supporting your back. Be sure that there are no major distractions (TV, cell phone, other people, pets, pizza on the way, etc.). Without any incense, candles, or other tools, sit quietly with your hands comfortably in your lap. Take one deep breath to start. Release all of the tension in your body starting in your head, jaw, and neck. Let your shoulders, arms, and abdomen relax. Let your legs, ankles, and feet relax.

Breathe normally. Focus on your breathing, feel it moving down your throat. Thoughts will come into your mind, but when they do, move back to focusing on your breathing. Do this for several minutes. When you feel ready, open your eyes and stand up. Walk around a little bit or even get some fresh air if you need to (meditation can often make you sleepy). Record your experience in your book of shadows. Once you've done this a few times without incense, candles, or tools, incorporate these things if they help you focus better.

*Exercise 2*

Do the meditation from exercise 1. Quiet your mind as best you can. When you get to the quietest point you can, open your hands, palms up. Feel the energy in the palms of your hands, it can sometimes feel like a slight weight. If you don't feel the energy there, press your palms together or rub them together, then pull them slowly apart. Bring them slowly together and then apart again. After awhile you will feel the energy there.

Focus on the energy coming from your hands, let the energy sit in the palms of your hands like pools of water. This energy is always in your hands, it's just a matter of taking notice of it. For several minutes, focus on the energy in your hands. When your mind starts to drift, focus on your breathing, then when your mind is quiet, begin focusing on the energy in your hands again. Just like your hands, your feet also emit this sort of energy, but because we mostly use our feet for walking, it can be a little trickier to feel the energy there. See if you can focus on the energy coming from your feet as well as your hands. When you feel ready, come out of the meditation. Record your experience in your book of shadows.

### *Exercise 3*

Go through meditation exercises 1 and 2. Take all of the time that you need. When you are ready, feel the energy in your feet and hands. Visualize roots growing from the bottoms of your feet, pushing through any flooring and into the earth. Feel the earth moving past your roots, cool and damp. Let your roots take hold in the earth, keeping you where you are, connecting you to the earth. There is no exchange here, no taking of the earth's energy and no giving of your own, there is just an open line of connection through your roots.

Continue visualizing this open line of connection, leaving you open to any messages or images that might come through. When you're ready, bring your roots back up and come back from the meditation. Record your experience in your book of shadows.

## Visualization Exercises

### *Exercise 1*

Sit down comfortably and take one or two deep breaths to relax your body. Just like with the first meditation exercise, relax all of your muscles. When you're relaxed and breathing normally, close your eyes. Imagine standing in your bathroom. Look at where things are. Where is your toothbrush? Where is your towel? Where is the light switch? In your mind, move to stand at the sink. Reach out with your dominant hand and turn on the faucet, just a little bit. Imagine what the handle feels like in your hand, how easy or difficult it is to turn it.

Hear the water slowly streaming out of the faucet. Turn it up higher, pay attention to turning the handle, what the water sounds like, what the light in the bathroom looks like. Cup your hand and put it under the running water. Imagine how warm or cold the water is in your hand. Bring your cupped hand to your mouth, take the water in and hold it in your mouth for a second. Is the water warm in your mouth or is it cold? If it's cold, does it hurt your teeth?

Swallow the water, feel it fall into your belly, refreshing you. Listen to the water running out of the faucet. Turn it up or down if you want. Keep focusing on the sound of the water, the sight of the light in your bathroom, and the feel of the water on your hand as you place it under the water, letting it pass between your fingers. Continue focusing on these sensations for as long as you can. When you're ready, open your eyes and come out of the visualization.

### *Exercise 2*

Once you are relaxed, take a few deep breaths and then breathe normally. See yourself standing under a leafy, green tree. It's a sunny day outside, but there's a cool breeze. The breeze moves against your skin, nice and cool while the sun warms your skin. The breeze moves the leaves of the tree. Listen to the sound the soft leaves make against each other. Take four steps forward into the shade of the tree. Feel how much cooler the air is under the shade. Look at the contrast between the shade of the tree and the sun falling on the ground outside the tree's shelter.

Smell the summer air, how fresh it is. Take it in, in a deep breath. Look at the trunk of the tree. It's bark is tough and cracked in places. Bring your gaze up toward the rising branches of the tree. You see that there's fruit hanging from the tree, your favorite fruit. Look at the color of it, the shape of it. Place your hand against the tree trunk, feel the old, rough bark. It's scratchy, but firm. There's a branch just to your right. You reach for it. The wood of the branch is smoother than the trunk. Simultaneously push with your feet against the ground and pull yourself up onto the branch with your arms.

Use your muscles, arms, hands, arms, and legs to pull yourself up onto the branch. When you can, sit down on the branch. It's not very comfortable, but another cool breeze comes by, hitting your skin. The fruit is hanging from a branch just above you, it's within arms reach. Reach your dominant hand forward and grasp the fruit. What does the skin feel like? What color is it? What is the shape? The fruit is warm from being in the sun, it sits in the center of your palm, warm and ready to eat.

If it has a peel, peel it, or if not, bite into the fruit. Focus on it's taste and texture. Is there a lot of juice from the fruit? Is it tart or sweet? Sit up in the tree for a little while and enjoy the fruit. Focus on the taste and texture of the fruit, focus on the warmth of the sun and the cool breeze, even focus on sitting on the branch and how it becomes uncomfortable after awhile. When you're ready, come out of the visualization.

*Exercise 3*

Take your time to relax your body, take a few deep breaths. When you're ready, close your eyes. See yourself sitting in the middle of a big, empty room. The floor is wooden, smooth, but is a little cold. There are a bunch of candles lit up around the room, casting a warm glow over the floor, walls, and ceiling. Look down around you and see that you are in a circle made of four separate objects. Look in front of you. You see that there is a small brass bell. Reach out with your dominant hand and pick it up. You find that even though it's a small bell, it still has some weight to it.

You lightly rotate your wrist to make the bell ring. Listen to the ring carry throughout the empty room. When the bell is nearly done singing, you place it back down on the floor with a small metallic *clunk* sound. Turn yourself, still sitting, to your right. Now in front of you, you see a pile of small cloudy, white stones. They're all small, but they're different shapes. You pick them all up in your dominant hand. Feel how cool they are, as cool as the floor on your legs. Move your fingers so that the stones move in your hands. Listen to the stones softly clack against each other.

Reach back toward the floor and place the stones back down. Listen to them tumble against the wood floor. Turn yourself again and look down at the floor. You see a small blue candle burning. You carefully pick it up and bring it closer to you. Feel the warmth coming from it. Does it have a scent? What does it smell like? Once your hands are warmed by the candle, you put it back down on the floor. See the light that it spreads onto the wood floor around it.

You turn yourself again to the right. Looking down at the floor you see a gray feather. It's no bigger than your hand. You pick up the feather. It's very soft and fine. Holding the feather in your dominant hand, you move it across the palm of your other hand. Feel how soft it is, how light. You place the feather back onto the floor with barely any noise at all. You turn, one last time, back to face the bell. You can go around the circle again, or come out of the visualization.

## Daily Dedication

This is my own, personal daily dedication. All you will need for it is one white candle and one black candle. If you can't get the candles or you're not allowed to have them, simply visualize them in your mind. It's your intent and the visual representation of balance that matters here.

Light both the black and the white candles. Breathe normally and relax. Quiet your mind as best you can. Once your mind is as quiet as you can get it, begin visualizing that your feet have grown roots. These roots reach down into the earth. The roots don't take or give, but they are open. When ready, begin the devotion.

"Beneath me, my roots stretch into the earth,

holding tight and searching.

Above me, I reach for air, rain, and warmth -

searching, embracing.

My veins run with the depth and mystery of the river.

My heart is the boiling, churning liquid fire beneath the mountain.

My bones are ancient branches of oak and redwood.

I breathe the promise of a warm breeze and the warning of a powerful wind.

Spirit of the earth, walk with me through the mountains;

Swim with me in the crashing tide of the sea;

Breathe deep with me to laugh and sing;

Warm yourself by the fire of my soul.

By stone, fire, breath, and tide -

Spirit of the earth, I open myself to you,

to live as one."

When you've finished the devotion, you can blow out the candles or continue your visualization and meditation. You can do this upon waking everyday or whenever you find time. The intent is what matters and sometimes, first thing in the morning, the only thing I intend is to make it to the coffee pot.

## Rituals

### *Raising a Circle*

First begin by cleansing the area. Using a broom or besom, sweep away any negative or distracting energies. Start from the center of your sacred space and sweep outward in a counterclockwise spiral. Once you've done that, come back to the center and do the same to the air with a large feather to get rid of any lingering negative or distracting energies. Start from the inside and move outward in a counterclockwise spiral (moving counterclockwise always undoes things, including energy). Then, use incense or smoldering herbs to consecrate the area. Start in the center of your sacred space and move in a clockwise motion outward (moving clockwise builds and creates energy).

Return to your altar once you've consecrated your sacred space. To ensure that negative and distracting energies don't manifest while you're working, use an herbal blend of ritual herbs to create a large pentacle over your sacred space. The herbal blend I usually use can be found in the Spells, Charms, and more section below. This herbal blend will go on the floor and over your altar. It doesn't have to be a thick line of herbs, just a sprinkling will do. This will protect you and keep out negative energies.

Back at your altar, use an instrument that you have to make music or just noise. This can be brief or go for as long as you like. I usually ring the bell that I have once or twice. Then light the black and white candles. This represents the vibration (music/sound from the instrument) that ran through our universe and brought life, death, light, and darkness into being (the light of the black and white candles). If there is any ceremonial incense or herbs to be burned for this ritual now is the time to light them.

Quiet your mind as best you can. Take whatever time you need to do this. When you're ready, begin the ritual.

### *Full Moon Ritual*

Raise the circle. When you're ready, stand with your feet flat on the ground. Hold your hands out in front of you or at your side at a comfortable height, palms up. Visualize roots extending out of your feet, reaching down into the earth. Feel them grab hold into the earth, not taking or giving, but leaving an open connection between you and the earth. Visualize small pools of water resting in the palms of your hands. In your mind, see the light of the full moon reflected in those pools of water.

Feel your connection from earth, to roots, to you, to water, to the full moon. You are another one of nature's conduits, connecting the earth to the moon. Once you are grounded and centered with these visualizations and open lines of connection, say the incantation.

" By bursting, silver light,

my heart and soul swell with the moon.

Hidden paths are illuminated,

ideas and dreams are made to revelations.

My eyes are shining silver,

full of epiphany and completion.

The abundance of the moon pulls at my heart

like the tides of the ocean.

By ancient light,

second sight grows clear.

Knowing – Seeing – Feeling – Being

Full and brightest moon -

dance with me around the fire;

gather herbs with me in the night;

Breathe in the shimmering air;

Swim with me in the silver sea."

Keep your mind quiet for as long as you can, keep the connections clear. Meditate and visualize as long as you want to. When you are done, give any thanks you wish to and blow out the candles. To bring down the circle, simply sweep away the herbal blend and leave the circle.

### *Waning Moon Ritual*

Raise the circle. When you're ready, stand with your feet flat on the ground. Hold your hands out in front of you or at your side at a comfortable height, palms up. Visualize roots extending out of your feet, reaching down into the earth. Feel them grab hold into the earth, not taking or giving, but leaving an open connection between you and the earth. Visualize small pools of water resting in the palms of your hands. See the shrinking light of the moon reflected in those pools of water.

Feel your connection from earth, to roots, to you, to water, to the waning moon. You are another one of nature's conduits, connecting the earth to the moon. Once you are grounded and centered with these visualizations and open lines of connection, say the incantation.

"Growing darkness, shrinking moon.

Energies wane, a promise of rest.

It's time to take the first step into shadow,

to turn within.

Reflect what little light is left.

Let the sand fall slowly through the fingers of moonlight.

Waning moon, balanced of dark and light -

Come sit with me beside the fire;

Feel the cool breeze upon your face;

Let's rest our heads upon the earth

and listen to the dark waves of the ocean."

Keep your mind quiet for as long as you can, keep the connections clear. Meditate and visualize as long as you want to. When you are done, give any thanks you wish to and blow out the candles. To bring down the circle, simply sweep away the herbal blend and leave the circle.

### *New Moon Ritual*

Raise the circle. When you're ready, stand with your feet flat on the ground. Hold your hands out in front of you or at your side at a comfortable height, palms up. Visualize roots extending out of your feet, reaching down into the earth. Feel them grab hold into the earth, not taking or giving, but leaving an open connection between you and the earth. Visualize small pools of water resting in the palms of your hands. See the darkness of the new moon reflected in those pools of water.

Feel your connection from earth, to roots, to you, to water, to the new moon. You are another one of nature's conduits, connecting the earth to the moon. Once you are grounded and centered with these visualizations and open lines of connection, say the incantation.

"Darkest moon,

wise and mysterious.

My soul dances with you in the shadows,

looking for answers.

Stepping within, embracing the dark,

to find what was lost, to find what was known.

Eyes growing stronger in the darkness,

feeling my way along the path.

In the blackest of skies, the stars lead the way,

illuminated in introspection.

I close my eyes as you close yours,

looking within, releasing, banishing, resting before rebirth.

Dark whispering moon -

Sleep with me beside the warmth of the fire;

Feel the ground stirring beneath us;

Listen to the owl's feathers on the wind;

Let us rest until the morning dew gathers on our skin."

Keep your mind quiet for as long as you can, keep the connections clear. Meditate and visualize as long as you want to. When you are done, give any thanks you wish to and blow out the candles. To bring down the circle, simply sweep away the herbal blend and leave the circle.

### *Waxing Moon Ritual*

Raise the circle. When you're ready, stand with your feet flat on the ground. Hold your hands out in front of you or at your side at a comfortable height, palms up. Visualize roots extending out of your feet, reaching down into the earth. Feel them grab hold into the earth, not taking or giving, but leaving an open connection between you and the earth. Visualize small pools of water resting in the palms of your hands. See the growing light of the waxing moon reflected in those pools of water.

Feel your connection from earth, to roots, to you, to water, to the waxing moon. You are another one of nature's conduits, connecting the earth to the moon. Once you are grounded and centered with these visualizations and open lines of connection, say the incantation.

" Eyes peeking open, trying to see.

Opportunities await as the shadows move to sleep.

Reaching forward in hope and growing light.

A time to prepare, a time to restore.

Stretching out, opening up.

My arms are wide, my face turns to the light.

Growing moon -

Help me build the fire anew;

Let's plant the seeds, that they may grow with us;

Breathe with me, take in the fresh night air;

Walk with me, into the rolling waves of the sea."

Keep your mind quiet for as long as you can, keep the connections clear. Meditate and visualize as long as you want to. When you are done, give any thanks you wish to and blow out the candles. To bring down the circle, simply sweep away the herbal blend and leave the circle.

### *Samhain Ritual*

Raise the circle. When you are relaxed and ready, kneel down with feet and hands both flat on the floor/ground. Visualize your feet and hands growing roots, stretching those roots down into the earth, grasping soil. There is no giving or taking of energy, only open connection between you and the earth. When you're ready, stand back up, facing your altar, while still visualizing the roots of your hands and feet reaching down into the earth. Once you are grounded and centered with these visualizations and open lines of connection, say the incantation.

"On this, the most sacred of nights, the veil is thin.

A time to remember, a time to celebrate the life that death left behind.

The harvest is done, the cold is seeping in.

Now we come in from the fields to find warmth by the hearth.

Long darkness is ahead, the cold a bitter promise.

Reap the rewards of long work done.

Tonight as our trees and fields die for the year,

the spirits of the dead walk with us,

whispering secrets, stories, tricks, and treats.

As the earth goes into its quiet slumber,

I too go within to find quiet warmth.

The trees grow dim and fall to rest.

I walk among them and whisper, 'goodnight'.

At home, a full harvest waits to last through the cold slumber of the earth.

Fill your belly, fill your heart, and feed the dead.

This night is on the cusp of change, embrace it with an open heart.

With the earth, I lie down to rest, to dream, and to prepare for rebirth."

Keep your mind quiet for as long as you can, keep the connections clear. Meditate and visualize as long as you want. When you are done, give any thanks you wish to and blow out the candles. To bring down the circle, simply sweep away the herbal blend and leave the circle.

### Yule Ritual

Raise the circle. When you are relaxed and ready, kneel down with feet and hands both flat on the floor/ground. Visualize your feet and hands growing roots, stretching those roots down into the earth, grasping soil. There is no giving or taking of energy, only open connection between you and the earth. When you're ready, stand back up, facing your altar, while still visualizing the roots of your hands and feet reaching down into the earth. Once you are grounded and centered with these visualizations and open lines of connection, say the incantation.

"Through the passage of darkness I've come.

Now I welcome the winter solstice, the longest and darkest of nights.

The wind blows cold into our bones,

reminding us of darkest times and the warmth of light that is to come.

From within myself, within the sleeping earth,

we've found answers, we've found our strength.

Now well rested, it's time to rise,

for at dawn we will turn our faces to the light.

The last night of great darkness, of rest and reflection,

thank you for the answers, for the time to be within,

for the time to ready myself to grow.

Spirit of the earth -

Tomorrow, light comes stronger,

but rest with me this last long night;

Sleep with me, the deepest of sleeps where dreams grow wings.

Tomorrow we rise, but tonight we celebrate the darkness by our hearth,

celebrate our passage through the night."

Keep your mind quiet for as long as you can, keep the connections clear. Meditate and visualize as long as you want. When you are done, give any thanks you wish to and blow out the candles. To bring down the circle, simply sweep away the herbal blend and leave the circle.

### *Imbolc Ritual*

Raise the circle. When you are relaxed and ready, kneel down with feet and hands both flat on the floor/ground. Visualize your feet and hands growing roots, stretching those roots down into the earth, grasping soil. There is no giving or taking of energy, only open connection between you and the earth. When you're ready, stand back up, facing your altar, while still visualizing the roots of your hands and feet reaching down into the earth. Once you are grounded and centered with these visualizations and open lines of connection, say the incantation.

"Just beneath the soil that is my skin,

my soul stretches out, ready to reach forward.

Pushing dirt between my fingers to reach the sunlight,

spring is on the rise.

Reborn from the ashes of winter,

the earth awakens, sprouting new hope.

Spirit of the earth -

Rise with me to fill our spirits with dreams and rebirth;

Walk with me toward the promising light of the sun."

Keep your mind quiet for as long as you can, keep the connections clear. Meditate and visualize as long as you want. When you are done, give any thanks you wish to and blow out the candles. To bring down the circle, simply sweep away the herbal blend and leave the circle.

### *Ostara Ritual*

Raise the circle. When you are relaxed and ready, kneel down with feet and hands both flat on the floor/ground. Visualize your feet and hands growing roots, stretching those roots down into the earth, grasping soil. There is no giving or taking of energy, only open connection between you and the earth. When you're ready, stand back up, facing your altar, while still visualizing the roots of your hands and feet reaching down into the earth. Once you are grounded and centered with these visualizations and open lines of connection, say the incantation.

"Reborn from the darkness of winter,

> the earth rises with new life and new strength.
>
> There is a warmth on the wind, the promise of summer.
>
> I breathe in the crisp spring air,
>
> drink in the bright green shoots that reach out of the cold soil.
>
> I run with the rabbit and the fox,
>
> leap into new life brought by spring.
>
> The time is now,
>
> the time to play, the time to plant,
>
> the time to sew.
>
> I will plant my dreams with the earth so that they may grow,
>
> bright and strong."

Keep your mind quiet for as long as you can, keep the connections clear. Meditate and visualize as long as you want. When you are done, give any thanks you wish to and blow out the candles. To bring down the circle, simply sweep away the herbal blend and leave the circle.

### *Beltane Ritual*

Raise the circle. When you are relaxed and ready, kneel down with feet and hands both flat on the floor/ground. Visualize your feet and hands growing roots, stretching those roots down into the earth, grasping soil. There is no giving or taking of energy, only open connection between you and the earth. When you're ready, stand back up, facing your altar, while still visualizing the roots of your hands and feet reaching down into the earth. Once you are grounded and centered with these visualizations and open lines of connection, say the incantation.

> "Songs of birds filter through the trees,
>
> lighting fires in our hearts, in our souls.
>
> Heavy now is the promise of love and fertility.
>
> The earth stretches wide, ready to create.
>
> Blossoms reach upward, caressed by the wings of the bee,
>
> filling my heart with hope and love.
>
> The sun is bright in the fields and trees.
>
> The forest beckons for company.

> Climbing the branches, rising higher,
>
> trying to catch up with my uplifted spirit."

Keep your mind quiet for as long as you can, keep the connections clear. Meditate and visualize as long as you want. When you are done, give any thanks you wish to and blow out the candles. To bring down the circle, simply sweep away the herbal blend and leave the circle.

### *Midsummer Ritual*

Raise the circle. When you are relaxed and ready, kneel down with feet and hands both flat on the floor/ground. Visualize your feet and hands growing roots, stretching those roots down into the earth, grasping soil. There is no giving or taking of energy, only open connection between you and the earth. When you're ready, stand back up, facing your altar, while still visualizing the roots of your hands and feet reaching down into the earth. Once you are grounded and centered with these visualizations and open lines of connection, say the incantation.

> "The earth breathes deep,
>
> full, content.
>
> The light shines on today,
>
> it's last hurrah.
>
> Dance with me, spirit of the earth,
>
> spin with me until we fall to the grass with heavy laughter.
>
> Let the sun lie warm on our faces,
>
> for soon it will walk away.
>
> Now, let us play,
>
> let us dance, feast, and celebrate.
>
> The day is long, our spirits are up,
>
> this is our time to laugh and have fun.
>
> The sun is bright and heavy now.
>
> It sings upon my skin in golden rhythm.
>
> Dance until nighttime comes,
>
> then dance some more until you can't anymore."

Keep your mind quiet for as long as you can, keep the connections clear. Meditate and visualize as long as you want. When you are done, give any thanks you wish to and blow out the candles. To bring down the circle, simply sweep away the herbal blend and leave the circle.

### *Lughnassadh Ritual*

Raise the circle. When you are relaxed and ready, kneel down with feet and hands both flat on the floor/ground. Visualize your feet and hands growing roots, stretching those roots down into the earth, grasping soil. There is no giving or taking of energy, only open connection between you and the earth. When you're ready, stand back up, facing your altar, while still visualizing the roots of your hands and feet reaching down into the earth. Once you are grounded and centered with these visualizations and open lines of connection, say the incantation.

"A cool breeze of autumn brushes through the grain.

The harvest begins.

Apples hang heavy, grains grow tall.

I stretch in the fading light, preparing for fall.

The time has come to harvest the fruits and the grains,

but also the wisdom and knowledge from the passing seasons.

There's work still to be done,

but a promise of rest is ahead."

Keep your mind quiet for as long as you can, keep the connections clear. Meditate and visualize as long as you want. When you are done, give any thanks you wish to and blow out the candles. To bring down the circle, simply sweep away the herbal blend and leave the circle.

### *Mabon Ritual*

Raise the circle. When you are relaxed and ready, kneel down with feet and hands both flat on the floor/ground. Visualize your feet and hands growing roots, stretching those roots down into the earth, grasping soil. There is no giving or taking of energy, only open connection between you and the earth. When you're ready, stand back up, facing your altar, while still visualizing the roots of your hands and feet reaching down into the earth. Once you are grounded and centered with these visualizations and open lines of connection, say the incantation.

"The harvest continues, the bounty grows.

Light and dark are balanced now,

but the days grow shorter again.

Spirit of the earth -

Thank you for your bounty;

Thank you for the warmth of summer;

Thank you for your beauty and strength.

As the light dissipates, so does the warmth.

Now is the beginning of endings.

This is a time for reflection, a time to learn.

A time to reap the knowledge gained,

collect the seeds for spring."

Keep your mind quiet for as long as you can, keep the connections clear. Meditate and visualize as long as you want. When you are done, give any thanks you wish to and blow out the candles. To bring down the circle, simply sweep away the herbal blend and leave the circle.

### *Menstrual Ritual*

Raise the circle. When you are relaxed and grounded, begin the ritual. Kneel down with one hand on the floor/ground and one hand placed over your uterus. Visualize roots growing once more from your feet and from the hand on the ground. Let those roots hold onto the soil while you focus on the energy coming from inside you. When you're ready, stand up at your altar with your roots still reaching into the earth from your hand and feet. Keep one hand over your uterus. Begin the incantation.

"By blood, sea, and moon the cycle begins again.

Through death, new life grows strong.

Beneath the powerful, gentle moon,

waves crash down while others take form.

The sacred cycle begins again.

The moon's blood seeps into the earth,

preparing the sewing of seeds.

Great, tumultuous change is promised.

> The journey begins again.
> Reaching, twisted pain and confusion,
> but from it comes strength, wisdom, resilience, life.
> Sacred blood, sacred wisdom,
> secrets of life run through these veins.
> Remember then, be here now, know what's to come."

Keep your mind quiet for as long as you can, keep the connections clear. Meditate and visualize as long as you want. When you are done, give any thanks you wish to and blow out the candles. To bring down the circle, simply sweep away the herbal blend and leave the circle.

## Spells, Charms, and more

### *Health and Healing Spells*

Steaming Brew of Healing

This brew is neither drunk nor put on the skin. Just put it in the bowl and breathe in the steam that rises from it.

**Ingredients:**

-3 drops eucalyptus oil

-3 drops lavender oil

-2 tsp. Chamomile

-2 tsp. Ginseng

-2 tsp. Dried lemon balm

-1/2 clove of garlic, sliced or whole

-A bowl sized cauldron, pot, or just a bowl

**Procedure:**

Charge each ingredient with your healing intent. Visualize yourself healing quickly. See bruises moving quickly through their colors and then finally disappearing. See wounds healing, closing up. See yourself breathing clearly, stomach settled, and fever waning. Put all of the ingredients into your bowl, pot, or cauldron, one by one. When all ingredients are in, pour hot steaming water into the bowl. Fill it however much you want.

Once the bowl is filled to your desire, lean over the bowl. Let the steam rise to your face, feel the warmth, and breathe it in. Continue your visualizations of a healing, healthy you. When you're done, simply pour out the brew. You can strain it and throw out the herbs or you can throw the whole thing outside into the earth.

Healing Soak

When you make this soak, first ice the wound. It's good to ice it for 20 minutes and then warm it for 20 minutes.

**Ingredients (for a gallon sized pot):**

- 1/4 cup rosemary
- 1/2 cup chamomile
- 1/2 cup lavender
- 2 sprigs of fresh basil
- 2 teaspoons eucalyptus oil

**Process:**

Add the ingredients while concentrating on your intent. Whether the soak is for yourself or someone else, imagine the wound healing and being protected from further damage. Warm up some water in a tea kettle or a separate pot. Once the water is steaming, **not** boiling pour the water into the pot with the herbs and oil.

Imagine healing energy coming out of your hands, hold your hands over the soak, projecting that energy and your intent into the soaking herbs. Do this for at least a few minutes, but you can continue to do so for as long as you like. If you want, you can say a few words to direct your intention or seek the help of a god/goddess/spirit. Soak the bruised/pulled appendage/muscle until the soak gets cold. Once the soak is cold, wipe the herbs off of the skin, then wrap it in a warm, dry towel.

Healing Jar

This spell jar is helpful for drawing healing energies to you or someone suffering from illness (physical and mental).

**Items you will need:**

- A jar of either moon water or sea water (if you can find a green or blue jar that would be even more beneficial)

- 6 drops of eucalyptus oil

- Bloodstone, moonstone, and/or hematite

- 9 pinches of garlic

- 3 Lemon zests

- 3 spoonfuls of mint

- One sprig of pine that will fit in the jar

- 3 drops of sandalwood oil

**Process:**

Do this on the night of a waxing moon to draw on the energies of the brightening, strengthening moon. Hold each ingredient in your hand, one by one. As you hold each ingredient, focus on your intent. Visualize them each drawing in healing energies.

Put the water into the jar, as you do so say, "Healing waters, wash away pain and illness." Continue your visualization. See the person who is suffering illness, be it you or someone else, becoming well again. Add the other ingredients, one by one as you continue this visualization.

Once all of the ingredients are in, take in the scent of the mixture, focus your energy into it. Place your hands over the opening of the jar. Continue to focus and say,

"By the light of the moon, by the power of earth

Now is a time for rebirth

Healing power flow to me

A river flowing to the mouth of the sea"

Chant this as many times as you wish, until you feel it is done. Close the jar with a tight fitting lid and then keep it near the bed of the one suffering the illness. Whoever the jar is for, they may repeat the chant every night before they go to sleep.

Once the person is healed, you can take the jar to a river or the ocean and dump it into the water. Be sure to give thanks as you do so.

Healing Spell

Helpful for getting past colds, speeding up the healing process of wounds, and feeling better physically.

**Items you will need:**

- Chamomile (at least 3 small handfuls worth, can usually be found in most health food stores)

- 3 drops eucalyptus Oil

- 3 Green Candles

**Process:**

Draw yourself a warm bath. Set up the green candles around the bath tub (on the floor is fine) and light them. Once the bath is drawn and you're in it comfortably, add 3 drops of eucalyptus oil to the bath. With your dominant hand, stir the water clockwise, 3 times. Smell the eucalyptus, close your eyes and breathe it in. If you have trouble detecting the oil, add 2 or 3 more drops. As you breathe in the scent, focus only on how it smells, how it makes you feel. When you are relaxed, sprinkle 3 small handfuls of chamomile into the bath with you.

Lower yourself into the bath, up to your neck, leaving your head above water. Take in the scents of the healing herbs. After a few relaxed moments recite the following as many times as you wish:

"Water soothe me

Fire warm me

Air revive me

Earth heal me"

Visualize your wounds healing faster, your sickness fading, whatever the ailment is leaving you faster, leaving you in good health. After you're done reciting the words and visualizing your healthy outcome, take a moment to relax completely in the bath. Continue to take in the scents of the herbs, meditate if you want to or continue to visualize yourself being healthy and feeling better.

When you are done, drain the water and clean out the bath tub (to make sure herbs don't clog up your pipes, place a thin wash cloth over the open drain/plug). You can shower to rinse off the rest of the herbs and oil or continue to meditate outside the bathtub.

### *Cleansing Spells*

<u>Self-Cleansing</u>

There's a lot out there about cleansing your sacred space, home, car, bedroom, and even your work area. But sometimes, we carry so much extra energy and it gets stagnant, and sometimes we need to cleanse ourselves. This is a simple self-cleansing that I've found works very well, especially during meditation.

**You will need:**

- Your favorite incense
- A large feather (I use a big turkey feather)
- Your meditation space (If you want)

**Procedure:**

I suggest doing this during meditation and during a waning or new moon. Ground and center yourself as best you can. Do what you usually do for meditation (light incense, candles, ring a bell, etc.). Light your favorite incense and breathe in the scent. Let it calm and relax you. When you are calm and centered, take the feather and use it to scoop and brush away all unnecessary, negative, and excess energy. I do this by moving it quickly and sharply very close to my body, through the air. Visualize the feather flinging and brushing away all unwanted energy, leaving the air in front of you clear.

Next, take your favorite incense and cleanse yourself with it. Let the smoke flow over your arms, your face (only very briefly, don't choke on it), your torso, legs, everywhere. Let the smoke fill the air around you with positive and constructive energy. Do this for as long as you feel necessary. When you are done, set what is left of the incense in an incense holder/burner. Continue with any meditation you may want to do, chants, etc.


Easy Space/House Cleansing & Protection

This is a cleansing and protection spell that me and one of my closest friends came up with a few years ago. It's simple easy, and only takes a few minutes (unless you live in a massive house or castle).

First, take an ordinary broom and sweep all dirt and debris out of your home. Then, using the same broom or a ritual broom, sweep up the stagnant and negative energies. Do this throughout the whole space/home. This brings up all stagnant and negative energies so that you can better clear them out.

Next, decide how you want to cleans your house or space. You can use a sage smudge stick, frankincense, or a mixture of sage and rosemary burning over charcoal. Open all of your windows and doors. Take the smoldering herb or incense around your home or space. Visualize all stagnant and negative energies being carried out with the smoke.

Once you've gone through the whole space/home with the smoke, make a small mixture of salt, rosemary, and sage. Sprinkle this mixture in all windowsills and across all doorways that lead outside the home/space (for example, if you have a door that leads to a porch, sprinkle the mixture outside the door on the porch). If you like, you can make a large mixture and put it around your whole property.

### *Love Spells*

## Love Oil

Great for drawing love energy to you. Wear it on the wrists and neck or use it to anoint a love spell candle. You can also use it as an offering to a love god/goddess.

**Ingredients:**

- 3 small lavender flowers

- 6 parts rose water

- 3 parts lavender oil

- 2 parts rosemary oil

- 1 part patchouli oil

## A Spell to Strengthen Love

This spell is to help strengthen love that is already present. It's very helpful for long distance relationships.

**You will need:**

- An herbal mixture of lavender, ground cinnamon, and chili pepper

- Two cinnamon sticks

- Three red candles

- Red or white ribbon

- A rose quartz (big or small, doesn't matter)

- Rose incense (if you can't find rose, lavender, or lover's incense will also do)

- If you have a deck of tarot cards, pulling out The Lovers card can help. Place it on your work area as you do this spell to help give it an extra little boost.

**Procedure:**

Light the incense and take in the scent. Relax your mind and body. Mix the herbs together, concentrating on strengthening the bond between you and your partner. Mix them with your finger, athame, or wand in a clockwise motion. Mix the herbs in this circular motion six times. Hold the rose quartz in front of you, whisper your partner's name to the stone and then lightly kiss the stone. Place the stone in the herbal mixture to the strengthen the herbs.

Reflect on your partner and all it is that you love about them. As you do this, light the three red candles. Visualize your partner, see them in your mind as clearly as you can. Think about their smile, laugh, embrace. Hold a cinnamon stick in each hand as you do this, one stick represents you, the other your partner. Focus on your intent and slowly bring the cinnamon sticks together. With either your saliva, a bit of your blood, or some rose or lavender oil, dampen the joined sticks (you can also use a combination of all three liquids if you want). Lay them in the herbal mixture.

Turn the sticks over in the herbal mixture until the herbs stick pretty well to it. As you do this chant the following six times:

"Our love is ever strong

By distance short or long

We find home in each other's hearts

Souls tied together from the start"

After the chant, use the ribbon to tie the sticks together. Wrap them tightly together, thinking about how precious and important your love is. You can tie the ends of the ribbon together, seal them with wax from the candles, or both.

Keep the tied sticks at the heart of your home or bedroom.

Note: If you find later that the relationship is not going well or if it is best to cut ties with your partner, simply disassemble the sticks and scatter the pieces to the four cardinal directions.

Self-Love Spell

This spell is great for finding love and respect for yourself. It can also help to calm and relax you.

**You will need:**

- A mirror

- 3 light blue candles (small tapers work best)

- 3 red or pink candles (again, small tapers work best)

- One of or a mixture of the following: lavender, rose petals, chamomile, and/or mint

**Procedure:**

Set the mirror up in front of you on a table, desk, your altar, or wherever you are comfortable. Place the candles around the mirror in a circle. Hold the herb(s) in your hands, feel the energy there, run the herb(s) between your fingers. As you do this, close your eyes and visualize yourself sitting where you are right at that moment. Visualize a green ball of energy at your heart Chakra (the center of your chest). See the light get brighter and more vibrant, mixing with the light from the candles, reflecting into the mirror and back to you. Breathe deeply, exhale slowly. Sprinkle the herb(s) onto the mirror and say:

"Love within, love without

Leave behind pain and doubt

I recognize the scars

so that I can breathe in the stars"

You can repeat this as many times as you want and even continue to use it with the visualization whenever you feel you're having a hard time.

*Note: If you're having difficulties with depression, anxiety, etc. spells can help, but they're not the end all be all answers. Be sure to seek out other forms of help as well. Just like money spells or weight loss spells, you have to work at the goal, job search and exercise for example.

Attraction Brew

This brew will help attract others to you and will help to attract you to the right places, a kind of "be in the right place at the right time" helper.

**Ingredients:**

- 1 tsp. rosewater

- 3 pinches rosemary

- 3 pinches cloves

- 3 pinches cinnamon

- 3 pinches lavender

- 1 drop of vanilla (oil or extract)

**Procedure:**

Charge all of these ingredients with your intent and your energy and then add them to a mason jar full of water (rain water or moon blessed water help give an extra power oomph). Brew this in the sun for three days and store in the fridge at night.

Strain out the herbs after the three days of sun brewing and store either in the fridge or a dark cabinet. Lasts about a month. Apply to the skin and leave to dry, don't wipe it off. Or you can use it in the bath or the shower. As you use it, visualize yourself attracting people with traits that you enjoy, not specific people, but the traits that they hold. Visualize yourself being in the right place at the right time.

A Spell to Bind Love

Use this spell to help detach yourself and your feelings from someone you once loved. Helpful in breakups and those pesky times of heartbreaking desperation when you consider going back to an ex.

**You will need:**

- One rose without the stem, just the flower (dried or fresh)

- Several rose thorns

- Black cloth

**Procedure:**

Perform during the waning moon

If you want to do this during circle, then build a circle, but it's not necessary. Invoke gods/goddesses or spirits if you wish. When you are centered and ready, press the thorns into the rose. As you do this, visualize this person having no hold over you (emotional, mental, or otherwise). Once all of the thorns are in the rose, begin to slowly wrap it in the black cloth. 13 times say, "(Person's name), I release myself from your hold, I bind your power over me, from this moment I am free, as I will it so mote it be".

Do any kind of grounding you need to when you are done. Keep the bound rose somewhere safe. You can keep it in your car, under your bed, hidden somewhere in your home, or you can carry it with you. When you feel that you don't need it anymore, bury it so that the earth may purify it.

Heartbreak Management Brew

This brew is great for helping you to manage your heartache. I created and used it after a horrible, painful break up that left me feeling broken. My thoughts were constantly cluttered with thoughts of him and I couldn't concentrate on my school work or my spiritual work. After using this brew for a while (I've found that brews take a little time to build up and become effective, it's not an instant pill that makes your feelings disappear) I found that I could focus more, I dealt with my feelings in a healthy way, I stopped blaming myself for his issues, and eventually I didn't need it anymore and I was back on my feet. (This whole healing process took about a month for me, but may be shorter or longer for others depending on their situation as well as other factors.)

**You will need:**

- A small bottle or jar (8 oz. is good)

- About 2 tsp. of marjoram (dried)

- 1 tsp. sage (dried)

- 3 drops of sandalwood oil

**The Process:**

Fill the bottle almost fully (leave about 2-3 inches empty at the top) with water (Blessed moon water or water collected from a powerful storm work best, but are not necessary, clean, fresh water works just fine). Add the ingredients while imagining your desired outcome. On your altar arrange four elemental candles (yellow-air-east, red-fire-south, blue-water-west, green-earth-north are what I use, but if you have your own method of candle-element representation do that).

Arrange these candles in a circle, put your altar candle and your brew in the middle with a crystal (size doesn't matter). Light the altar candle and make your intention for the brew very clear. Center yourself and clear your mind as best you can. State your intention, something like, "With this brew I manage my heartache in a healthy, progressive way", state this several times out loud.

Then light each elemental candle while saying, "By the powers of earth, air, fire, and water I consecrate this brew to aid me with managing my heartache."

Visualize what it is that you want to achieve with this brew. Visualize yourself getting work done without distraction. Visualize yourself doing your normal, everyday activities without being hindered by pain and heartache. Visualize yourself facing the pain, the problem, and the heartache with an open mind and seeing the situation from an objective view point. Visualize yourself accepting and loving yourself, embracing your strengths and your weaknesses and growing from it.

Take as long as you need during the visualization. When you are done put out the candles and then leave the bottle in the window for 3 days and 3 nights to absorb the energies of the sun and the moon (you can also leave it outside if it is safe there). You can end the ritual thanking any gods/goddesses or spirits that you worship if you choose to do so.

Use the finished brew in the shower, pour a little over your skin, let the water carry it over you to be absorbed by your skin. Or put it in the bath, meditate with it while in the bath, do more visualization here. You can also put some of it over your heart Chakra at any time, don't dry it off, let it dry on its own. Being a constantly on-the-go college student, I would do this on my way out the door.

### *Banishing and Protection Spells*

Banishing Spell

A simple, helpful spell to keep unwanted people away from you. Once the spell is done, continue to restrict any contact with the person.

**What You'll Need:**

- A picture of the person you are banishing

- Black salt (feel free to add some black pepper for a little extra oomph if you want, but it's not absolutely needed)

- A bowl

- One large black candle

**Process:**

Do this spell over the course of the waning moon, leaving the last night of the spell for the night of the new moon. Place the picture of the person you want to leave you alone in the bowl. Every night, light the black candle and center yourself. Once you're centered, sprinkle some of the black salt onto the person's picture. As you do this, say,

"Away from me, out of my sight

Leave me be, every day, every night"

You can chant this for awhile if you want, or just say it once. Extinguish the candle. Do this every night up to the new moon. On the new moon, the picture should be covered by the black salt so that you don't see the image anymore. Once it's done you can take the black candle and the bowl with the black salt and the buried picture outside (at night) and bury it deep in the ground or simply throw it away, but do not look at the picture. Some people like to keep their spells for awhile before they dispose of them to make sure the spell worked, that's fine too.

**Remember: Spells are great helpful tools, but it's always wise to take your own action. If someone is bothering you or threatening you, you should tell someone. No one has the right to make you feel threatened, violated, or unsafe in anyway.

Protection Charm

**Items Needed:**

-Salt

-A small bit of tiger's eye

- A bit of Ivy, dill, rosemary, basil, and pine

-And one small blue bag or pouch

**The Procedure:**

Before putting the charm together, center yourself. Once you are grounded and centered, focus on your intent. Start to place the ingredients into the blue bag, one by one. As you put each ingredient in, visualize your intent. Visualize that you're (or whoever you're making the charm for) surrounded by a protective light, almost as if you're/they're inside a bubble. Visualize good things entering the sphere around you/them and bad or negative things bouncing off of the outer shell of the sphere.

Once all items are in the bag, hold it in your hands and continue to visualize. Then say, "Keep me safe, keep me protected - from danger and from harm". Chant this as many times as you like (I usually do 9 or 13, but that's just personal preference). Then, if you follow a specific path you can ask the God(s), Goddess(es), the universe, the great spirit, etc. to bless the charm.

You can keep this in your car, your purse, on a key chain, at home, wherever you want it.


Nightmare Prevention Charm

Helps to prevent unwanted dreams. I cannot say how it works for night terrors, I used this to help me stop dreaming of an ex-boyfriend after we broke up. It took a few days for it to kick in, but once it did it was very helpful.

**You will need:**

- A small black bag or pouch

- One small black candle (small tapers from most occult shops work best)

- One small green candle ("                                               ")

- 1 to 2 tea spoons of chamomile

- one citrine stone (small ones are best)

- one lepidolite stone (small ones are best)

**Process:**

Burn the black candle for a while, half way down at the most while reciting the dreams to be prevented. Visualize the dreams kind of poofing into smoke and floating away. Burn the green candle the same as the black, but this time recite how this charm will help you grow (ex: This charm will remove all mental stress and hindrances in my dreams so that I may grow) Visualize yourself sleeping soundly with positive or silly dreams that do not hurt or hinder you.

Once the wicks of both candles are cooled put them into the black pouch. Charge the chamomile, citrine, and lepidolite with your energy and your intent to rid yourself of these nightmares and to promote positive dreams. Add these ingredients to the pouch. Close the pouch and hold it close to you, visualizing positive dreams. I visualized myself standing behind a giant dream catcher where nightmares bounced off and disappeared. Take a few moments to do this visualization. If you want to, ask a god/goddess or spirit for their help, state why you've made the charm and what you wish to accomplish with it. After you've done this, give thanks for the assistance (a simple "Thank you" or even an offering).

Keep the charm under your pillow at all times. When you feel you don't need it anymore you can store it away or bury it so that the earth can purify it. I put mine away and brought it back out when I had nightmares about the next ex-boyfriend and it worked just the same. I kept this charm for four years and it worked for four years. Eventually when it did stop working, I buried it.

Banishing Herbal Blend

Use this in spells to banish unwanted visitors, people, pests, and even bad habits. You can carry some in a pouch with you along with a piece of what you want banished (a bit of the person's hair, some tobacco, etc.).

**You will need:**

-3 parts black salt (to make at home, simply mix regular salt and incense ashes together)

-3 parts black pepper

-1 part powdered garlic

*Helpful Miscellaneous Spells*

Ritual Herbal Blend

This is a really easy to make herbal blend that you can use for rituals. You'll probably find most if not all of these ingredients in your kitchen.

**Ingredients:**

Equal parts

- Salt

- Sage

- Rosemary

- Black Pepper

**How to use it:**

Mix these ingredients, knowing that they will bring your circle protection and cleansing as well as create a sacred space for you to do your work. Once you've swept and cleansed the circle of negative and distracting energies, simply walk the circle, spreading the herbs on the floor/ground (much easier clean up on hardwood or linoleum if inside). It doesn't have to be a thick line, but just so that you can see where the boundary of the circle is. Then continue on with your ritual as you normally would.


House Blessing Spell Bottle

**Items You Will Need:**

- A bottle or jar

- 2 parts Allspice

- 2 parts Rosemary

- 3 parts Chamomile

- 2 parts Lavender

- 1 part Sage

- 2 parts Peppermint

- 2 parts Black Pepper

- A bit of hair, saliva, or blood of every person and pet residing in the home (you can always use 3 drops of rose water in place of this ingredient, just focus on that person and their presence in the home as you add it).

**Process:**

Add all ingredients together, if someone in your home wants to help then you can make it together. Focus on your intent as you add the ingredients, visualize a safe, healthy, and happy home. Once all ingredients are in the bottle, focus your energy into the bottle (you can do this during a ritual if you choose to do so, but you don't have to).

When it's completed, hold it close to your heart, continue to visualize your desired outcome, focus on your intent. Take as long as you need. When you're done, place the bottle in the heart of your home, this can be your bedroom, kitchen, living room, or anywhere else you find that you and your housemates spend a lot of time and enjoy each other's company.

Self-Confidence Spell

If you need to find your inner strength or boost your confidence, this spell can help you out.

**What You'll Need:**

- A clear quartz crystal
- A rose quartz
- 3 acorns
- 3 white candles

**Procedure:**

Set the clear and rose quartz before you, side by side. Place the acorns with them. Place the three white candles in a half moon shape around them, leaving the open side toward you. Focus on your intent. See your intended outcome of embracing your inner power, your confidence rising. Light the white candles, as you do say, "By the brightest of days and the darkest of nights, let my inner power rise by this light."

Focus on the light reflected in the stones, visualize that light growing larger and brighter into a warm white light. Touch your fingertips to the stones and acorns, feel the warmth there, feel the tree inside the acorns. The acorn is small, but it holds the strength of a forest. Feel the forest inside yourself, know the strength and the potential that you hold inside yourself.

As you touch your fingertips to the stones and acorns, visualize the white light running up your hand and your arm, filling your soul, high lighting the strength within. Three times, chant,"By the brightest of days and the darkest of nights, let my inner power rise by this light."

You can continue to chant this as long as you like, in times of stress or anxiety you can also use this chant to help you out.

Energy Charm

This charm is helpful in drawing energy to you. Great for when it's hard to find the energy to do things, stay awake, or wake up. Perfect for those "zombie" days.

**Items Needed:**

- Mandrake (***Do not ingest, poisonous!***) - 3 Pinches

- Lemongrass - 3 Pinches

- Dill - 3 Pinches

- Either a red or orange drawstring bag (small)

- A small bit of quartz crystal

**Procedure:**

Place the quartz crystal in the sun for one day, take it out of the window or bring it inside once the sun has gone down. This will charge it with the sun's energy. Lay the ingredients in front of you and focus on your intent. Hold each herb and the stone in your hand, one by one. Visualize your intent. See yourself having energy and doing everything you need to do. Visualize yourself not growing tired right away, getting out of bed, ready to do what you need or want to do. Continue these visualizations until you feel calm and centered. When you are ready, place each ingredient into the drawstring bag. As you do this, say:

"God of passion and energy, hear this rite,

Fill me with your warmth and light"

You can chant this for as long as you like.

Carry the charm with you wherever you go, continue to do activities to help boost your energy (exercising, drinking lemongrass tea, etc.)


A Spell for Memory

If you need help remembering things, be it anything from writing that awful term paper or paying your bills, try this spell.

**You Will Need:**

- one yellow candle (small tapers work best)

- one of or a combination of the following herbs: Eyebright, Hawthorn, Rosemary

- A large bit of Citrine or Clear Quartz

- Water in a clear glass

**Procedure:**

Sit down comfortably at your altar, a table, a desk, or even on the floor. Light the yellow candle and place the stone in front of it so that it catches the light from the candle. Focus on that illuminated stone. Imagine that your mind is very much like this stone catching the light. It holds the light within it, just as your mind holds information and memories. Continue gazing at the stone for some time, let your mind settle and focus only on the stone. This stone, with it's reflected light, is the only thing that exists. Relax. Begin to visualize yourself remembering all that you need to, see yourself recalling any and all information that you know. You can even envision your mind as a sponge that soaks up knowledge and information, making it easy to recall anything you need.

When you are completely relaxed, hold the herb(s) in your hand. Continue your visualization, put that energy into the herbs. Sprinkle the herbs, clockwise, around the candle and stone. As you do this say:

"By earth, I make my memory solid

By fire, I make my memory strong

By air, I make my memory precise

By water, I make my memory clear"

Dip your fingertips into the water, then spritz the candle, stone, and herbs (not too much, you don't want the candle to go out). Continue to visualize and meditate as long as you like. When you are done, store the candle away or keep it to do the spell again if you wish to repeat the spell for a few nights (some people like to do spells more than once). Sleep with the stone under your pillow for a full cycle of the moon.

Money Charm

Here is an easy money charm for anyone who need some extra cash.

**You will need:**

- An avocado seed

- A small silver coin, a dime will work just fine

- A bit of paper money (anything will work, in the past I've used a single dollar bill, but it is said that the higher the bill you use in a money spell, the more money it will bring you)

- Green string

- A green candle

**Process:**

Make sure your avocado seed is completely dried out. If you have the whole pit of the avocado, place it in a window that gets a lot of sunlight to help dry it out. It should peel and you'll see that it has two halves. You will only need one half, but this gives you the opportunity to make two money charms, one for you and one for a friend, or you can keep the other half to make another money charm later if you lose the first one.

Place the silver coin on the flat, inside part of the half-pit. Press the coin into the pit and focus on your intent. Then, wrap the coin and half-pit tightly in the bill. Again, focus on your intent, make sure your intent is clear. Then, tie the green string around the charm tightly, make sure that it holds the bill around the half-pit/coin.

Knot the string so that it cannot fall off of the charm. Then pour some of the hot green wax from the candle onto the knot to seal it. When the wax is cool and dried over the knot, hold it in your hands. Visualize your desired outcome clearly. You can carry the charm with you or keep it with your wallet when you're home. If you have a business you can keep it there (with your finances, near the cash register, etc.). You can also put it in a small drawstring bag and carry it with you on your bag or with your keys.

Honor Candles

Honor candles are great for honoring those who have passed on. It is a way to thank them for what they've given us in life and honor their path through this cycle of life. Honor candles are really very simple and don't require an actual ritual, but you can set one up during ritual if you want to.

For an honor candle, find something for an offering. Your offering should be something personal to the person that you are honoring. For instance, I always use coffee grounds when offering my Nana who died in 2010. I use coffee grounds because she and I would always drink coffee together, a lot of coffee.

To do an honor candle, light a black candle and put the offering in a small dish in front of the black candle. You can meditate here for a while if you want, think about the person who has passed, thank them for what they've given you in this life. I usually let the candle burn for about twenty minutes, then once it's blown out and cool, I'll store it away to use again later for an honoring if I want to do it again later, then I put the offering out in my garden.

Death is never easy, but we can honor those who have passed and live our lives with the lessons that we've learned from those who have moved on.

# Part Three – Recommended Reading

The following are books that I have read, enjoy, and reference in my own practice. I recommend giving all of these books a good once over. I've rated them in an out of 5 star system, giving my own opinion on each book. While some books are expensive, most libraries are happy to order books in from other libraries for you.

*A Modern Guide to Witchcraft by Skye Alexander*

A newer book, but the first I've seen that is not tied to any religious or spiritual practice. Just Witchcraft. **5/5 Stars.**

*Power of the Witch by Laurie Cabot*

An interesting read. It has a lot of good theories. It also explains the science of magick very well. The only drawback is that it's pretty sexist against men. Expresses that all women are witches, but leaves men out of it for the most part. **3/5 stars.**

*Wicca and Witchcraft for Dummies by Diane Smith*

Explains magick and spells very well. A very good book for anyone interested in Wicca. Only drawback is that they use Wicca and witchcraft as interchangeable terms. **4/5 stars.**

*Wicca: A Guide for the Solitary Practitioner by Scott Cunningham*

Another book that explains magick and spells well. Also another good book for those interested in Wicca, but not just a witchcraft book. **3.5/5 stars.**

*Living Wicca by Scott Cunningham*

Also good in explaining magick and spells, but is mostly a Wicca book. What is nice about it is that it get's passed the 101 stuff. **3.5/5 stars.**

*The Circle Within by Dianne Sylvan*

One of the best Wicca books I've ever read that get's beyond the 101 stuff. Not so good for just witchcraft though. But overall I'd give it **4/5 stars** (if that's the kind of stuff you're looking for).

*The Good Spell Book by Gillian Kemp*

Lots of great spells and interesting tidbits about the Romani people. **4/5 stars.**

*The Fortune Telling Book by Gillian Kemp*

Amazing for divination. Excellent book. **5/5 stars.**

*The Complete Tarot Kit by Susan Levitt*

By far the best kit and book about tarot that I have ever read. It's pricey, but it is absolutely 120% worth it. So much information and history, easy to read and understand. It also comes with two decks of tarot cards. This is what I used to teach myself how to read tarot cards, I still use the cards and book today, 12 years later. **5/5 stars.**

*The Complete Book of Incense, Oils, and Brews by Scott Cunningham*

Very good book, full of excellent spells and recipes. **4/5 stars.**

*The Green Wiccan Herbal by Silja*

While it has Wicca in the name and has some Wiccan beliefs in it, this book is full of very good spells and very good information. **4/5 stars.**

*Crystal Ball Gazing by Uma Silbey*

Great for beginners. Easy to read and understand. **3.5/5 stars.**

*Simply Tea Leaf Reading by Jacqueline Towers*

Helpful to get started with tea leaf reading. Contains a non-exhaustive list of symbols and their meanings. **3.5/5 stars.**

*How to Read the Tarot by Sylvia Abraham*

An interesting little book to help add to your tarot collection. Has it's own card's meanings, but also a list of good spreads that are easy to construct and understand. **3.5/5 stars.**

*Drawing Down the Moon by Margot Adler*

If you're looking for a religion to go with your witchcraft, this book can prove very helpful. Adler goes through a good (non-exhaustive) list of religions and spiritualities that use witchcraft in their religious practice. Also a good anthropology read. **4.5/5 stars.**

# ABOUT THE AUTHOR

Jamie Weaver is mostly a fiction author, however, this non-fiction guide to witchcraft is a book that she was happy to write in order to share her knowledge and experiences with other people who may have interest in witchcraft and spirituality. Her other work includes a book of poetry titled *Storm in my Teacup and other poems* and a fiction novel titled *Anything* which explores the blessings and curses of love, loss, and fighting for your dreams. You can learn more about Jamie's work and her current works in progress by visiting her author website:
https://jweaverwrites.wixsite.com/jamieweaver

Printed in Great Britain
by Amazon